Classic Super BIKES

FROM AROUND THE WORLD

MAC McDIARMID ●

Classic SuperBIKES

FROM AROUND THE WORLD

P
PARRAGON

Page 1 — Possibly the most eye-catching British vertical twin, the limited production Rickman Interceptor.

Page 2 — MV Agusta 750S America, based — if only loosely — on the most successful grand prix 500 ever built.

Page 3 — The ultimate Bonnie — 1965 Thruxton model.

First Published in Great Britain in 1995 by Parragon
Units 13-17, Avonbridge Trading Estate
Atlantic Road, Avonmouth, Bristol BS11 9QD
United Kingdom

Designed and produced by
Stonecastle Graphics Limited
Old Chapel Studio, Plain Road, Marden
Tonbridge, Kent TN12 9LS United Kingdom

© Parragon 1996
  Reprinted in 1997

All rights reserved. No part of this publication may be reproduced, stored in a retrieval system, or transmitted in any way or by any means, electronic, mechanical, photocopying, recording or otherwise, without the prior permission of the copyright holder.

ISBN 0 75251 017 7

Printed in Italy

Photography credits

All photographs by Mac McDiarmid except:
Martyn Barnwell/**Classic Bike:** pages 18-19,
    22-23, 24-25, 40-41, 68-69
Roland Brown: pages 76 (top), 77, 80-81
Jack Burnicle: pages 86-7, 94-95
David Goldman: pages 32-33, 48-49
Patrick Gosling: page 61
Kick Start magazine: pages 72-73
Phil Masters: pages 82-83, 84-85
Don Morley: pages 10-11, 34-35
Oli Tennent: pages 8-9, 14-15, 60, 70-71
to all of whom, many thanks.

Contents

Honda CB750: perhaps the most revolutionary machine of a revolutionary era. Once, only factory racers were built like this.

Introduction

·························

Only two things are common to the motorcycles on the following pages. Most obviously of all, they each have two wheels. And, with rare exceptions, they have telescopic forks and paired rear shock absorbers. This was, in essence, the twin-shock era, bounded fore and aft by plunger and monoshock rear ends.

Yet it is engines which most distinguish the period. As befitted the austerity of the post-war years, the 'fifties began with the single – four-stroke or two-, as the people's engine. Although there were what we might call 'bespoke singles' (like Velocettes and Norton's Inter), riders of greater means or ambition sought four-stroke twins. Most were parallel, the descendants of Alfred Turner's 1937 Triumph Speed Twin. A few, notably Harley-Davidson and the Vincent in their very different ways, were in Vee configuration. Others, even more rarely, were opposed.

Multis barely got a look-in. The Danish Nimbus, the last surviving relic of countless car-type longitudinal fours, failed to survive the decade. Ariel's Square Four was an heroic, imposing, but largely irrelevant cul-de-sac. Indeed, it was the commercial failure of machines like the Square Four which did much to dissuade the British motorcycle industry from further such enterprise.

Meanwhile the two-stroke, DKW's valiant efforts aside, was effectively confined to the role of humble commuter. Most were smoky, slow, and – even by the standards of the time – unreliable. In 1950 they were certainly not the sort of fare to justify inclusion in any catalogue of 'Classic Superbikes'.

Three revolutions in three countries changed all this. Italy (with a little help from West Germany's NSU) turned the concept of high-revving, multi-cylinder four-strokes into screaming metal – but

Series C Vincent Rapide: rare, expensive and fast. These attributes made it definitely a Superbike long before the expression was coined.

exclusively on the race track. Meanwhile a comparable transformation was set in motion when East Germany's MZ utterly transformed ideas of two-stroke capabilities. Again, this revolution was confined to competition. But it redefined human ideas of what was possible. And it is people, let us not forget, who create motorcycles.

It was left to the Japanese, who entered the 'fifties as motorcycling nonentities, and the 'sixties as a two-wheeled joke, to put both sets of ideas onto the street. The 'sixties was the decade in which Japanese manufacturers stole a little, borrowed a lot, and innovated massively, to transform the face of motorcycling. By design they proved that complexity could go hand-in-hand with reliability; and by the third of our revolutions – in manufacturing – they proved that both could be achieved at an affordable price. In 1969, the transverse multi and the high-performance two-stroke twin were exotic. Just six years later they had begun to establish themselves as the norm.

A few manufacturers copied the Japanese approach with, at best, transient success (although others, notably in Italy, have since succeeded). Of the rest, most who ploughed their own furrow dwindled or died. BMW's opposed twins continue

to survive in their iconoclastic way, yet even they have resorted to multis, albeit of an independent bent. Moto Guzzi's Vee twins hang on to life rather more grimly. Harley-Davidson have 're-invented' the past, and sell hugely on an anti high-tech ticket. Ducati continue to create two-wheeled Ferraris to evocative, if relatively small-scale, effect. And the British motorcycle industry disappeared. Of all the manufacturers on the following pages, only nine, at most, continue as producers of 'superbikes'.

Since our quarter century ended in 1975 the two-stroke twin has effectively been sidelined by emissions legislation. Strokers survive on the street either as slightly delinquent sports machines, or – echoes of the 'fifties – as utilitarian lightweights. In competition they remain supreme – an anachronism the racing authorities must surely soon address.

On the dominant, four-stroke front, much of what has happened since has been in the detail – four (even five or eight) valves per cylinder; the almost universal adoption of water-cooling; fuel injection (but surprisingly rarely); and above all a transformation in the quality of chassis, suspension and brakes. But the foundations for all of this were laid here, 1950 to 1975; twenty-five years that changed the face of motorcycling.

Ducati 750SS factory racer: Fogarty's 916 is a direct descendant. Liquid-cooling, multi-valves, fuel injection and – above all – chassis refinements would come later.

Harley-Davidson WL45

·······················

*I*t's fitting that the first 'Classic Superbike' should wear the tank badge of the world's oldest surviving motorcycle manufacturer. Since their foundation in 1903, Harley-Davidson have been doing things resolutely the American way – or perhaps 'Milwaukee way' is more apt.

Harley-Davidson, of course, is synonymous with the Vee-twin, a layout they first adopted in 1909. That first twin, with the now-familiar 45 degree included angle, displaced 61cu.in (999.6cc) and was said to be capable of almost 60mph from its 7bhp. It was a notable success, and the company grew rapidly. By 1914 the factory had mushroomed to 297,000 square feet, and during World War I no less than 20,000 Harleys saw military duty.

But in 1995 Harley-Davidson are the iconoclasts of world motorcycling – a situation little different from the '50s. This particular model, the WL45,

SPECIFICATION: HARLEY-DAVIDSON WL45	
ENGINE	739cc side-valve Vee-twin
HORSEPOWER	24.5bhp @ 4600rpm
TRANSMISSION	3-speed
FRAME	tubular single cradle, rigid rear end
BRAKES	drum/drum
TOP SPEED	68mph

began life in 1929, continuing in production with only relatively minor modifications until the arrival of the 'K' Model in 1952. For an entire generation, this was *the* Harley-Davidson, as American as apple pie.

In 1929, the WL was the first of a new generation of side-valve 'flathead' Vee-twins. The '45' denotes the capacity in cubic inches, equivalent to 739cc. In 1930 it was joined by a sister model, the 74-inch VL. Almost on their own, this duo saw Harley through The Depression, for no significant new models were to be developed during six years of economic strife. Of literally hundreds of American bike manufacturers, only Harley and Indian survived, as industry-wide production dropped from 32,000 to 6000 units by 1933. One Harley response was the three-wheeled 'Servi-Car' a cheap delivery and police vehicle powered by the WL engine, which lasted until the mid-'70s.

In 1936 new models began to emerge, with an

'For an entire generation, this was <u>the</u> Harley-Davidson, as American as apple pie.'

80-inch (1310cc) side-valve twin and the legendary 61-inch ohv Knucklehead. But the WL, along with Indian's side-valve 750, remained the Harley mainstay, an increasingly integral part of American culture. (And elsewhere – WLs were actually manufactured in Japan under licence, bearing the Rikuo name). Not surprisingly it was to the WL (suffixed 'A' for Army) that the American military turned during World War II. Of 90,000 Harleys 'enlisted' almost 89,000 were good ol' 45-inch WLA V-twins. It was a long way from 1903, when William S Harley, Arthur Davidson and two other Davidson brothers produced just three motorcycles in a shed measuring 10 foot by 15.

Hostilities over, Harley set about uprating their range, first with the 74-inch, alloy-headed Panhead, complete with hydraulic lifters; then with the first of the Glides, the Hydra Glide. Yet still the WL plodded on, its girder forks, side-valve engine and rigid rear end a growing anachronism but its sheer indestructibility continuing to be prized. Eventually, in 1952, it was replaced by another machine which was to become an American legend. For the K-model not only featured hydraulically damped suspension at both ends, but was later to become the XL Sportster.

The WL is – and was for most of its life – a crude, heavy machine better suited to the American Prairies than any road with bends. Cruising all day at 60mph on a long, straight road, it is in its element. But with 550lbs of momentum, poor brakes, minimal suspension and a wide gap between its three gear ratios, anything else is hard work. Even setting off is a knack, thanks to the WL's foot-operated 'suicide' clutch.

The WL was, even in 1950, a motorcycling dinosaur. But if it was slow, outdated and cumbersome, it was also strong as an ox and almost indestructible; a tough old workhorse that delivered the bacon. The superbikes that were to come would be something else altogether.

Thundering along the straightaways has been the Harley forte since long before the invention of recreational 'cruising'.

Never powerful and certainly not very fast, the side-valve 45-inch 'flathead' Harley, with girder forks and rigid rear end, helped keep America mobile for a generation.

Nimbus 750-Four

·······························

*F*ours are nothing new. Since the early years of the century, a host of manufacturers have shoe-horned four-cylinder engines into road-going motorcycles; FN in Belgium, Henderson in the USA, countless others around the world, and even, briefly, Brough in the UK. And the most enduring of these was a small company from Copenhagen, Denmark – Nimbus.

In 1918 the company's founder, Peder Fisker, launched his first production machine, the 'Stovepipe' Nimbus. Loosely based on the FN, it was exquisitely made, with swing arm rear suspension only one of several innovative features. Although the years brought a few diversions, the basic layout was to remain until the very last Nimbus; four cylinders longitudinally in-line, with shaft final drive.

Reminiscent of the Austin Seven car engine, the softly-tuned Nimbus was the opposite of the fours which would later dominate the Superbike era.

The early Nimbus was very expensive to produce, and the onset of the Depression demanded that economies be made. The MkII, introduced in 1934, was much more utilitarian. Gone was the rear suspension, and the brazed tubular backbone frame gave way to a curious affair of riveted steel strip. The MkII had Fisker's own telescopic forks, however, several months ahead of BMW's and probably the first on any motorcycle.

The new 750cc engine, too, was advanced: a SOHC four, with inclined valves and hemispherical combustion chambers. The camshaft was bevel driven, whilst the crankshaft ran in just two huge ball bearings. The big-ends were shell-type. A three-speed gearbox transmitted the Nimbus' modest power by shaft to the rear wheel.

This was never likely to amount to a performance machine. Cooling, with four close-set cast-iron cylinders each heating the other's air, was always poor. The valvegear is open to the elements. The two-bearing crank would flex if revved hard. And the single 26mm Nimbus carburettor is probably the smallest ever fitted to a four. Power in standard trim (and the Nimbus was never much tuned) was 22bhp at a leisurely 4500rpm. Whilst this was good for brief bursts up to 60mph, sustained flat-out cruising evidently warped the cylinder head 'like a banana'.

The Nimbus was the last of the in-line fours which graced the early years of motorcycle development. By the 'fifties, it had become an anachronism.

'This was a machine for riding with dignity, never panache.'

But 1934? Yes, and not really. Fisker was, as a matter of policy and temperament, opposed to change for change's sake. So the MkII continued in production, in much its original form, until 1958. Any part from a 1956 Nimbus will almost certainly fit one 20 years older, and vice versa. Such changes as were made were minor, mainly to instruments, brakes and other ancillaries.

To the end of its life, the MkII retained its rigid rear end. In solo use the ride, like almost everything about the machine, was deeply idiosyncratic. This was a machine for riding with dignity, never panache.

Yet it was, in Denmark at least, a moderately successful motorcycle. In all, something like 12,000 MkIIs were produced. It was rugged, economical (60-plus mpg), maintenance was simple, and it hauled a sidecar with ease. The MkII became popular with Danish tradesmen and military alike.

Even after motorcycle production ceased in 1958, the factory continued to manufacture spares. Although this was mainly to honour its obligations to the military, even in the late 'sixties it was

possible to have a Nimbus built from new parts to special order.

But was it a superbike? Not really. Sure, it was a four, which might otherwise mark it as special. But everything about the Nimbus, far from looking forward to the days of high-revving sports bikes, harked back to an age of motorised gentlemen's carriages. It was an utter anachronism, surviving into the Space Age but almost Edwardian in character. Yet, if nothing else, it shows that there is nothing innately sophisticated about multis. As such, it is a useful book-end to an era that ended with fours of an altogether different ilk.

SPECIFICATION: NIMBUS 750-FOUR	
ENGINE	air-cooled 746cc SOHC longitudinal four
HORSEPOWER	22bhp @ 4500rpm
TRANSMISSION	3-speed
FRAME	Riveted steel strip
BRAKES	drum/drum
TOP SPEED	60mph

Scott Squirrel

'The lightness and simplicity of the two-stroke twin were potent features.'

The Scott Squirrel only just creeps into this volume's frame of reference, but its background warrants mention in any book on motorcycling. Alfred Angas Scott, founder of the Scott motorcycle company, was one of the great innovators of motorcycling's early years. It was Scott who patented a form of caliper brake as early as 1897, a fully triangulated frame, rotary induction valves, unit construction, the first motorcycle kick-start and much, much more.

Most of all, Scott pioneered the liquid-cooled two-stroke parallel twin with which the Scott name will forever be associated. Yet for all this ingenuity, once Scott had hit on their favoured engine layout, they stuck to it through thick and thin until the company collapsed almost half a century later.

The epitome of Edwardian endeavour, as well as being a gifted inventor and engineer, Scott was an accomplished artist and painter. As early as 1904 he patented his first engine, a vertical twin two-stroke, inevitably – which he fitted onto his Premier bicycle (and occasionally into a small boat, the Petrel).

In 1908 he began motorcycle production, initially using the Bradford facilities of the Jowett brothers, later famous for their cars. The first Scotts used a patented frame which was to survive substantially unchanged until 1930; and a new 333cc liquid-cooled engine.

Although the engine shortly grew to 450cc, with later versions displacing 498 or 596cc, all were of the 'classic' Scott design; two-stroke, using overhung two-bearing crankshafts with the drive taken from a central flywheel. This layout allowed for a large diameter flywheel which was effective without excessive weight. Coolant was circulated through the large honeycomb radiator (another Scott patent) by natural thermo-syphon effect, rather than pumped.

By the time the company moved into new premises at Shipley in 1912, the 'yowling two-strokes' had a string of competition successes behind them. Scott's twins had proved, 55 years before the Japanese demonstrated it again, that the lightness and simplicity of the two-stroke twin were

potent features. As well as innumerable wins in trials and hill-climbs, Scott machines won the Senior TT in 1912 and 1913.

Early Scotts used a simple, but effective, two-speed transmission. The first three-speeder, the legendary Flying Squirrel, appeared in 1926. This was produced in both 498 and 596cc forms. However, four years earlier Alfred Scott himself had died at the age of just 48, from pneumonia contracted after a pot-holing trip. With his departure much of the initiative went out of the company, which was having increasing difficulty competing with the ever-more powerful four-strokes. In 1931 the official receiver was called in.

A Liverpudlian, Albert Reynolds stepped in to save Scott, but the under-capitalised company never fully recovered. Plans for a 650cc twin never

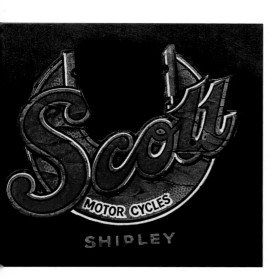

By the 'fifties, Scott's once-revolutionary design was as quaint — and dated — as the Shipley factory's logo.

SPECIFICATION: SCOTT SQUIRREL	
ENGINE	liquid-cooled 596cc two-stroke twin
HORSEPOWER	30bhp @ 5000rpm
TRANSMISSION	3-speed
FRAME	tubular steel triangulated twin cradle
BRAKES	drum/drum
TOP SPEED	85mph

Production of the 596cc rigid framed Flying Squirrel continued after the war, initially with girder forks and later with Dowty telescopics. In 1949 coil ignition replaced the more familiar Lucas Magdyno. However, sales were poor and production ceased less than 12 months later. The example pictured is from 1950, one of the very last machines to leave Scott's Shipley works.

However, the story did not quite end there. In 1956 a new generation of Scotts were built in small numbers, basically Flying Squirrel engines in a contemporary swing-arm frame. Sadly the project was short-lived, as was the later Silk, essentially a Scott in a sophisticated racing-type Spondon chassis. Exquisite though it was, it was under-powered and expensive, and flickered only briefly.

reached fruition. An even more exciting prospect, Bill Cull's three-cylinder two-stroke design, originally of 747, later 986cc, was shown at the 1934 Olympia Show but never reached production. 1938 brought a 596cc Clubman's Special whose 90mph-plus top speed aroused considerable interest, but the war intervened.

In the 'twenties, thanks to the energy and imagination of Alfred Scott, liquid-cooled two-stroke twins such as this were the machines to have. But the last Squirrels were little more advanced than those of a generation earlier.

Indian Chief

·······················

For many years the Indian name evoked American motorcycling quite as vividly as Harley-Davidson does today. Founded by George Hendee and Oscar Hedstrom in 1901 – even earlier than Harley – the Springfield, Massachusetts company's first model was a 1³/4 horsepower single. Yet just a decade later an Indian ridden by OC Godfrey became the first overseas machine to win the Isle of Man TT. Numerous other competition successes followed, particularly in the uniquely American sports of flat-track and board racing. There were laurels, too, in long-distance ordeals, where men like Erwin 'Cannonball' Baker achieved almost legendary status.

If it looks like a Harley, that's because it did a similar job over the same terrain. The 1308cc side-valve engine was as rugged as it was crude, but failed to meet the performance expectations of the post-war generation.

Nor were Indian averse to novelty. They offered early forms of electric start and rear suspension before World War I. They even built engines with four valves per cylinder – although the 'Big Valve' two-valve 1000 of 1919 proved to be faster. In the early 'twenties they built an experimental overhead camshaft 500, although this never raced and it was on a sidevalve Indian that Freddie Dixon placed third in the 1923 TT. The last racer to come out of the factory, a 1948 'Big Base' 750 V-twin, was still going strong on American half miles into the late '60s. More remarkable still, the same Indian Scout that had set a speed record in 1931 was last seen racing at Sacramento in 1968.

Despite this endeavour, Indian fell into the first of many financial crises as early as 1919. The machine which rescued them then was to form the backbone of their range for decades. The 600cc Scout stood out in a market dominated by heavyweight 1000cc machines (although a 1000cc Indian Chief followed). It was light (300lbs), smooth and agile, with a full electrical system, all-chain drive and three-speed gearbox. Nonetheless the Scout retained the traditional 'suicide' foot clutch and hand-operated gearchange. And although it wore two brakes, both acted on the rear wheel. It wasn't until 1928 that a Harley became the first American motorcycle to 'pioneer' the front brake.

On acquiring the Ace motorcycle company in 1927, Indian began production of a range of in-line fours which were to become almost as uniquely Indian as its twins. Although the Vee-twin is now thought of as the definitive American engine configuration, for many years a host of US manufacturers, notably Henderson, produced such behemoths. Paradoxically, the Danish Nimbus featured on page 10 was the last of this breed.

In 1940 both the twins and the fours gained sprung rear ends, nine years before Harley were to follow suit with the Hydra-Glide. Yet the 'forties also saw an ill-advised attempt to build vertical twins in the Triumph mould. Indian's elderly designs certainly needed modernising, but this was not the way. The vertical twins proved to be unreliable and unpopular, imposing a huge financial strain on the troubled Indian company.

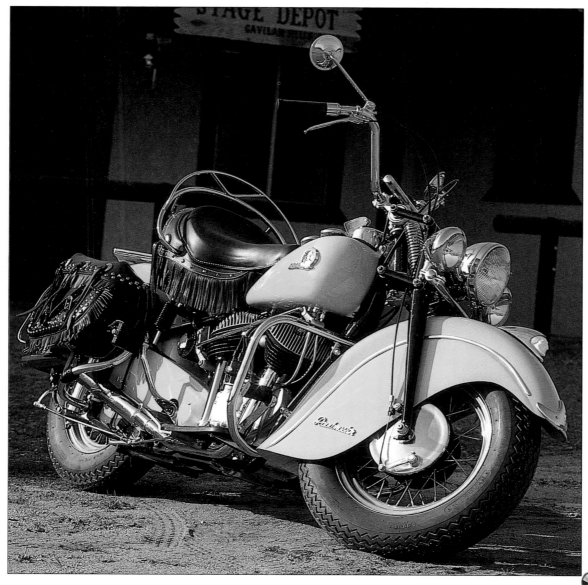

*'The same
Indian Scout
that had set a
speed record in
1931 was last
seen racing at
Sacramento in
1968.'*

Early Indians toyed with overhead cams and four valves-per-cylinder. But by the 'twenties, let alone the 'fifties, Indian's early taste for novelty and experiment had long worn off. Ironically, Harley now prosper recreating the same 'iron horse' image.

In 1949 the 1200cc Chief was enlarged to become the 1300cc juggernaut pictured. However, quality was poor and sales sluggish, and in August 1953 the once-mighty company ceased motorcycle production. Instead, the Indian name degenerated into a sales device for re-badged British machines. At one time or another, AJS, Douglas, Excelsior, Matchless, Norton, Royal Enfield, Velocette and Vincents have all worn the familiar Indian Chief tank badge. Indeed, the engine of the Rickman Interceptor featured on page 64 had originally been destined to wear an Indian timing cover in the USA.

At the end of the 'seventies, yet another tribe of 'Indians' appeared. Assembled at the Italian Italjet factory, using Italian cycle parts but British Velocette Venom engines, these were the brainchild of Floyd Clymer, of Clymer workshop manual fame. When this venture folded after Clymer's (and

Velocette's) death, the Indian rights passed to a Los Angeles company who embarked on the first of two failed attempts to sell Taiwanese mopeds under the old Springfield name. Yet for all these undignified failures, the Indian name continues to hold a resonant attraction to motorcyclists. It is currently being linked to a Vee-twin machine being designed for Indian by John Britten in New Zealand.

SPECIFICATION: INDIAN CHIEF	
ENGINE	air-cooled 1308cc OHV Vee-twin
HORSEPOWER	50bhp @ 4800rpm
TRANSMISSION	3-speed, hand change
FRAME	duplex tubular steel cradle
BRAKES	drum/drum
TOP SPEED	90mph

Norton International

·····················

*I*f the Manx Norton was one of the most famous racing motorcycles of all time, then the International must be one of the most legendary roadsters. In fact, they were substantially the same machine, differentiated at the factory by the name scribbled on the job-card. 'Manx' simply meant racing specification, whilst 'Inter' referred to a roadster with lights. Nonetheless, many Inters found themselves stripped down for racing. Over half a century before Suzuki's GSX-R750 re-worked the theme, these were the 'race replicas' of their day.

The precursor of both was the Norton CS1, a 490cc 'fast tourer' which itself derived from the works machine on which Stanley Woods had emphatically led the 1927 TT until retiring with clutch failure. Fortunately for Norton, Alec Bennett

A bevel-driven overhead camshaft (the works racers later had two) was the most exotic touch to the 500cc Inter engine. The system demanded far more expert setting-up than chain-driven valvegear designs.

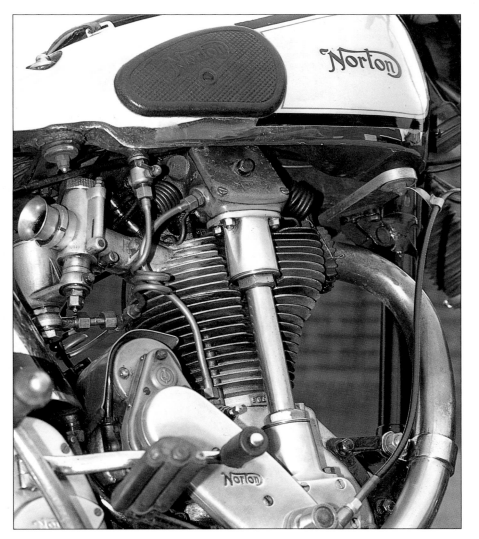

rode a second machine rather more circumspectly, winning at an average speed of 68.41mph.

Overhead camshafts were new to Norton, whose previous racing success was achieved with pushrod engines. But the success of overhead camshaft designs from Velocette and Blackburne spurred Walter Moore to design the classy 'cammy' Norton single. When a production version was unveiled at the 1927 motorcycle show, the 'CS' of the name stood for 'camshaft' for, like the Inter and Manx which were to succeed it, the CS1 boasted an overhead camshaft driven by shaft and bevel gears.

However, by 1929 the new Norton racer was already being eclipsed, and Arthur Carroll set about the redesign which was to create the immortal Manx. A road-going version was first offered to the public in 1932, and the Inter was born. Almost at once it was tested at 100mph, an astonishing speed for a half litre machine at the time. Buoyed by the continued track success of its factory racing siblings, the International became the definitive sporting machine of its era.

'The
International
became the
definitive
sporting
machine of its
era.'

The example pictured is an unrestored 1952 'Garden Gate' International, one of the last before the legendary Featherbed chassis gave the cammy single a brief new lease of life.

Factory versions of the cammy Norton engine went on to win no less than seven Senior TTs in the 'thirties, raising the lap record from 76 to over 90mph in the process. 350cc versions of the same engine were no less successful. Yet perhaps the biggest accolade for the roadster came in 1939. With the factory pre-occupied with military affairs, Norton's TT effort centred around six privateers riding – what else? – stripped-down Internationals.

The 'thirties, undoubtedly, was the Inter's heyday. But just as the factory Norton racers had to fight hard to remain competitive after 1950, so the Inter felt the weight of competition from a new generation of machines. Not the least of these came from Norton itself. The 497cc Dominator launched in 1948 offered a comparable level of performance in a machine that was far cleaner, easier to maintain, and cheaper to produce. Of all the methods of driving overhead camshafts, bevel gears are the most intricate, which is why belt or chain drive is preferred today. Inters, moreover, retained their messy exposed valve springs to the end.

The Inter, along with the rest of the Norton range, had acquired telescopic forks from 1948. The next development came in 1953 with the introduction of an alloy cylinder barrel, improved gearbox, better brakes and – above all – the renowned Featherbed frame. Whilst this marked a quantum leap in the Inter's roadholding, the same was true of Norton's sporting twins. Nonetheless, stripped-down Inters were still popular amongst racing privateers, but even here a threat was looming. 1952 had brought Clubman's TT victories for BSA's emerging Gold Star in both 350 and 500cc classes. Although the Featherbed Inter resumed it's rightful place in claiming the 1953 500cc Clubman's TT, the Gold Star went on to sweep all before it. From then on, the Norton International faded quietly away, last being listed in the 1958 Norton catalogue at £303.2.10d.

More than any other design, Norton were associated with highly-tuned overhead cam singles. The 'Inter' was a rare chance to use one on the road.

SPECIFICATION: NORTON INTERNATIONAL	
ENGINE	air-cooled 497cc OHC single
HORSEPOWER	up to 46bhp
TRANSMISSION	4-speed
FRAME	'Garden Gate' tubular steel cradle
BRAKES	drum/drum
TOP SPEED	up to 120mph in racing trim

Sunbeam S7/S8

·····························

'This 'magnificent' creation was overweight, slow, fairly thirsty, looked weird, didn't handle and soon attracted a reputation for unreliability.'

This was to be the jewel in the crown of post-war British motorcycling, and it had the full weight of the giant BSA Group behind it. During the war years, BSA acquired two things; the Sunbeam name, and a captured German BMW R75 outfit. As the war was coming to a conclusion, BSA recognised that they needed a flagship model, and set about creating one under the Sunbeam banner, which had always been associated with 'gentlemen's conveyances'

Erling Poppe, essentially a car man, was the project's chief designer, and the resulting machine adopted much from automotive technology. It borrowed even more from the BMW – frame and running gear layout, dynamo, brakes, wheels and tyre sizes, and the concept of a shaft-drive twin with the gearbox behind the engine. Unfortunately the one vital German piece that was not purloined turned out to be the Sunbeam's downfall.

BSA might also have pinched BMW's flat-twin engine, but that would have been a little too obvious. Instead, Poppe designed a new powerplant, still a twin with the crankshaft fore-and-aft, but now with cylinders in-line astern rather than opposed. Astonishingly, this was the only new overhead cam motorcycle engine to go into production in post-war Britain until the (even more ill-fated) Hesketh in 1981.

Poppe also designed a new four-speed gearbox with bevels allowing the kick-start to be sited much less awkwardly than the Bee-eM's. Unfortunately this meant ditching the proven crown-and-pinion final drive in favour of an underslung worm gear. Apparently the choice was made because the BSA Group, which also produced Daimler and Lanchester cars, was familiar with making this type of drive!

BSA leaked details of the new machine liberally, as well as presenting one to Field Marshal 'Monty' Montgomery of Alamein. Such was the sense of anticipation, and so great the curious crowd, that at the 1948 Motor Cycle Show the Sunbeam stand collapsed under the weight!

Yet this excitement was sadly misplaced. Early prototypes of what was actually a fairly free-breathing and potent engine had already shown that final drive worm gears lasted no more than 5000 miles. Rather than address the real problem, Sunbeam designed an entirely new cylinder head to reduce power. The resulting 23.6bhp, allied to a dry weight of 435lb, left the S7 serious under-motivated.

There was more. An early batch of S7s rushed out to South Africa had to be recalled when vibration proved too severe. Later examples had rubber-mounted engines (and a corrosion-prone

---

SPECIFICATION: SUNBEAM S7/S8

ENGINE	air-cooled 487cc OHC tandem twin
HORSEPOWER	26bhp @ 5800rpm (S8)
TRANSMISSION	4-speed
FRAME	tubular twin loop
BRAKES	drum/drum
TOP SPEED	80mph

flexible exhaust section) – and the handling, on those fat 4.75 x 16 tyres, was distinctly odd (and gave the S7 the look, according to a contemporary report, of 'a motor trapped between two doughnuts').

Billed as 'The world's most magnificent motor cycle', the S7 went on sale in 1947 at the very high price of £222. This 'magnificent' creation was overweight, slow, fairly thirsty, looked weird, didn't handle and soon attracted a reputation for unreliability. Only around 2000 S7s were made before 1949 when the heavily reworked 'sports' S8 and S7 De Luxe were introduced.

Both received numerous engine changes (notably a bigger oil capacity), and the S8 adopted BSA A10 wheels and forks but retained plunger rear suspension. The S8 was about 5mph quicker and

30lb lighter than its predecessor. Ridden prudently, it proved reliable, but pedestrian – that flawed final drive was more dependable, but it still soaked up power. Arguably it is the 'dignity' of its performance (and the snootiness of Sunbeam dealers), as much as anything aristocratic in its design, that gave the Sunbeam the aura of gentleman's carriage.

Still, the 'Beam began to sell, and by December 1952, 10,000 had been built. From then on sales steadily declined, and the range was dropped when BSA and Triumph merged in late '56. The attempt to produce the first post-war superbike had failed.

Quiet, smooth and clean, the shaft-drive S8 'gentleman's carriage' was the nearest thing to a British BMW.

Although the only British overhead cam roadster to go into production between the war and 1981, the Sunbeam's development – and its potential – was fudged.

Vincent 1000 Series C

·······················

'Every red-blooded motorcyclist aspired to owning one, yet very few could.'

They still speak of the ghosts of Vincent Vee-twins thundering down the Stevenage by-pass. Long before the expression was coined, 'the world's fastest standard production machine' was in every way a superbike; fast, technically advanced and brutally good-looking.

Although now associated most of all with *that* engine, Vincent had originally used proprietory power plants from the likes of Blackburne and JAP. After a duff batch of JAP engines was foisted on him at the 1934 TT, Phil Vincent resolved never to be dependent on outside engine suppliers again.

Although Vincent was himself a brilliant and innovative designer, the resulting engines were the work of the ingenious Australian, Phil Irving. Irving first produced the Meteor, a high-camshaft 499cc single capable of 90mph in sports 'Comet' form. Then came the big 'un, essentially a brace of 499cc Meteor top-ends arranged in a 47 degree Vee on a common crankcase. This became the Series A, dubbed the 'plumber's nightmare' due to an abundance of external oil pipes.

Breathtaking though it was, the Series A had several problems – the wheelbase, at 59 inches, was ponderously long; and, worst of all, no proprietory clutch or gearbox could handle its prodigious torque.

The result was the post-war Series B Rapide. The transmission was uprated by the use of an ingenious self servo clutch, and a new gearbox was designed in-unit with the engine. The latter was not only sturdier than its predecessor, but shorter. A radical new 'frame' – basically a box joining steering head and rear sub-frame, with the engine as a stressed member – allowed Vincent to dispense with

Vincent horsepower tested the technology of the time — in transmissions, brakes, tyres and suspension — to the absolute limit. Maintenance had to be similarly painstaking.

front downtubes, further shortening the wheelbase. When the Rapide arrived in 1946, this stood at a relatively nimble 56 inches.

Meanwhile the Vee was increased to 50 degrees, allowing both the use of a standard Lucas magneto, and better location for the carburettor float bowls.

The Rapide was better in every way than the Series A, and with 45bhp and 110mph, at least as rapid. The first Black Shadow, in 1948, claimed 55bhp on 'pool' petrol – or a staggering 100bhp on racing methanol. In 1949 the Series C arrived, with Vincent Girdraulic forks in place of Brampton girders (but retaining Vincent's novel Series A triangulated rear suspension), and began re-writing the record books the world over.

Irving's post-war engine design survived the next nine years, from Series B to Series D, fundamentally unchanged. Produced in touring, sports and racing guises as the Rapide, Black Shadow and Black Lightning respectively, its performance remained unequalled by any production motorcycle until well into the 'seventies. Every red-blooded motorcyclist aspired to owning

one, yet very few could; the hand-crafted Vincent was always prohibitively expensive.

Times became particularly hard in 1954. Vincent's response, on the one hand, was to manufacture NSU mopeds and commuter machines under licence at the Stevenage factory. More humiliating still, these were marketed under the Vincent name.

His other response was to ask his customers, the Vincent Owners' Club, what they wanted from the forthcoming Series D. For any manufacturer this is always a risky practice, and so it proved. Series D duly arrived in the form of the Black Knight and Black Prince, successors to the Rapide and Shadow respectively. Some details, notably coil ignition, were better. But both models were fully enclosed, like giant black scooters. The public was horrified.

Series D was quickly reintroduced with 'proper' naked Vincents, and almost everyone was happy. But this costly U-turn was the factory's last major act. Sales were tumbling and costs rising, and in 1955 Vincent closed their gates for the last time. The big black Vee-twins are no more. But the legend lives on.

A top speed of 125mph made the Black Shadow comfortably the fastest machine of its age — indeed, nothing very much faster would appear for 20 years.

SPECIFICATION: VINCENT 1000 SERIES C	
ENGINE	air-cooled 998cc OHV Vee-twin
HORSEPOWER	55bhp @ 5500rpm
TRANSMISSION	4-speed
FRAME	backbone box-section, engine as stressed member
BRAKES	Double drum/double drum
TOP SPEED	125mph

Moto Guzzi Falcone Sport

Like Triumph's twins, in one form or another this quintessential Moto Guzzi single spanned the entire 25-year range of this book. Yet even when the 'fifties began, it was not essentially new. The Italian company's very first prototype machine, in the days when they were known as Guzzi and Parodi, was a horizontal single not a great deal different from the Falcone. The year was 1920.

For its time, the single was very advanced. It used a short-stroke engine of 498.4cc, with a single overhead cam driven by bevel gears in the manner of later Manx Nortons. Most radical of all was its four-valve head. However, by the time production versions were announced in December 1920, both the company name had changed – to the familiar Moto Guzzi – and the machine's specification had been downgraded. It now used push-rod operation of just two valves, and went on sale in 1921 as the Moto Guzzi *Tipo Normale* – Standard Model.

The original four-valve design later appeared as a racing machine, winning first time out in the 1924 *Circuit del Lario*. Thus began a long tradition of Moto Guzzi track success, mostly based on light, aerodynamic singles. From 1947 until the rise of NSU in 1954, their 250 single was well-nigh

unbeatable; and in taking the world title from 1953–57, their 350 single showed the virtue of simplicity in defying the mighty MV and Gilera fours. Yet at the other extreme, there was the awesome 500cc Vee-8, a supercharged transverse four as early as 1930, and numerous other twins, triples and fours.

Guzzi's roadsters, however, took the simple route. When the Falcone was first introduced in 1950, it was little more than a tuned version of the 1949 Astore tourer, which itself had much in common with the original *Normale* of 1921. A flat single with the same 88 x 82mm short-stroke layout, compared to the Astore, the Falcone had a bigger carburettor, higher compression ratio, hotter camshaft and lighter con rod. Power had risen from 19bhp at 4300rpm to 23bhp at 4500. A characteristic of both engines was their large external flywheel, a means of achieving considerable flywheel effect (necessary in a single), without an equally considerable weight penalty.

The Falcone dispensed with the Astore's legshields, also adopting flatter handlebars and more rear-set footrests. In keeping with its sporting pretensions, the rear springs were both shorter and stiffer than before. Although the rear suspension

If it doesn't move, paint it scarlet! Falcone was an antique, even in the 'fifties, but a glorious one. Note the low engine, reminiscent of later Aermacchis, and the 'upside down' front forks: very few motorcycling novelties are actually new.

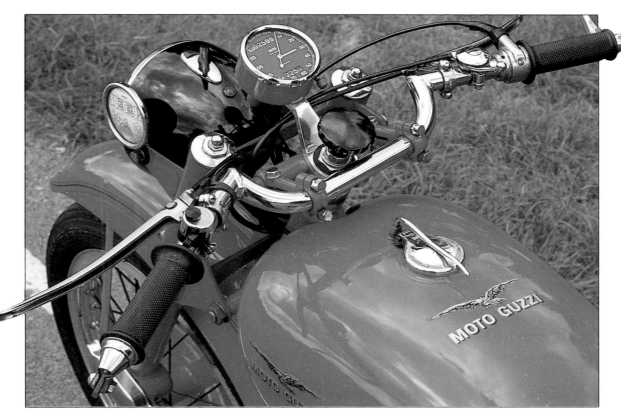

The Mandello eagle has probably graced a greater variety of engine layouts than any other European logo.

used a triangulated swing-arm, the general design dated from 1928 and employed a crude friction damping system. The springs, four in all, live in a box under the engine – not unlike Harley-Davidson's current Softail 'retro' design.

Equally 'modern-but-dated' were the telescopic front forks. These were of the 'upside-down' type, adjustable – yet first appeared on the 250cc Airone of 1947. Meanwhile the frame, an odd collection of steel tube and plate, splits in two in the manner of several much later Bimotas.

In 1953, when the Falcone Turismo replaced the Astore, Guzzi officially christened the existing model the Falcone Sport. Of all the many versions of the post-1950 single, a genuine Sport is the rarest, most prized – and most imitated. Collectors beware!

For all its ancient origins, the Falcone went well for an early 'fifties machine. Quicker than all but a handful of the most raucous British sports singles, it was smooth, comfortable, with a plush and well-damped ride which belied its dated suspension.

Yet as the years passed, Guzzi singles changed little. Increasingly old-fashioned, they were mainly bought by civil and military authorities in their native Italy. A new, but broadly similar, Nuovo Falcone was launched for police and military use in 1969, and offered to the public two years later. It sold poorly and was dropped in 1976.

SPECIFICATION: MOTO GUZZI FALCONE	
ENGINE	air-cooled 498cc OHV flat single
HORSEPOWER	23bhp @ 4500rpm
TRANSMISSION	4-speed
FRAME	tubular/plate, twin downtubes
BRAKES	drum/drum
TOP SPEED	85mph

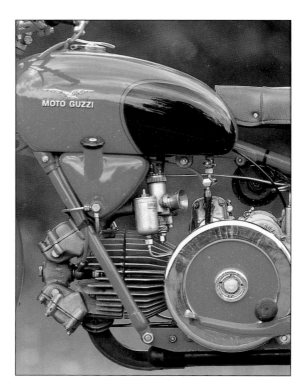

'For all its ancient origins, the Falcone went well for an early 'fifties machine.'

Ubiquitous Guzzi outside flywheel design allowed considerable flywheel effect without the penalty of heavy internal flywheels.

Ariel Square Four

·························

'It was smooth, effortless and, above all, imposing.'

$\mathscr{I}$n the days before Italy, and then Japan proved otherwise, mounting an in-line four cylinder engine in anything but a touring motorcycle posed an insurmountable problem: mount it longitudinally, and the bike was too long; transversely, and it was unacceptably wide. So any four with sporting pretensions required a different layout.

This was the thinking of a young engineer in a small machine shop in Dulwich, South London. His response? A 497cc overhead cam square four. His name? Edward Turner, later to find fame as the designer of Triumph's immortal Speed Twin.

Turner hawked his engine around several manufacturers until Jack Sangster of Ariel decided to give it a chance. The resulting prototype, housed (with room to spare) in a 500 'sloper' frame, was the sensation of the Olympia motor cycle show. The year was just 1930.

The 497cc engine, essentially two vertical twins on a common crankcase, comprised paired transverse crankshafts, geared together at their centres. A chain on the right side of the engine drove both a magdyno and the single overhead camshaft. The wet-sump crankcases split horizontally. It was an astonishingly light and compact design which delivered most of what Turner had set out to achieve. The whole machine weighed only 330lbs.

Throughout its life, however, the 'Squariel' had one major weakness. The cylinder head was prone to distortion, as the rear cylinders sat in the heat shadow of the front ones, and the provision of cooling air around the head was always marginal. On early examples this was exacerbated by inadequate lubrication. Early attempts to race the

Undoubtedly still a Superbike in the 'fifties, the 1000cc Squariel was even more so when this girder-forked example was built in 1937. Post-war changes, including telescopic front suspension and plunger rear, were insufficient to keep the big four competitive.

Rear cylinders of the Square four engine (above) tended to run hot, so it was only suited to low-stressed touring use, for which its top gear pulling power was ideal.
The Squariels pictured left are a rigid-framed 1946 4G model and a 1957 4G MkII with plunger rear end.

four, albeit in supercharged form, were plagued by problems of heads warping. Although a normally-aspirated version managed to take the coveted Maudes Trophy by covering 700 miles in 668 minutes, overheating and the inefficient 'cruciform' inlet tract would always impose a limit on the Squariel's performance.

When the machine went on sale it cost £70. A year later, a bored 597cc version was displayed at Olympia, but shortly afterwards the Depression hit the British economy. In 1937 a less ambitious range of fours was launched. Available in both 597 (the 4F) and 997cc (4G) form, these featured push-rod valve actuation, vertically-split crankcases and, partly to suit sidecar use, very much heavier flywheels. The 4G produced 38bhp at 5500rpm. In 1939, a clever form of plunger rear suspension was added.

After the war the 600cc Squariel was dropped, and by 1948 the 1000 had developed telescopic forks. Thanks largely to a new light alloy cylinder head and block, weight was down by some 33lb, but this was still a 500lb machine – and it still ran very hot.

1954 brought the final Square Four, the MkII 'four-piper'. Power had risen to 42bhp, but plunger rear suspension was retained in an age when

swinging forks were becoming commonplace on machines of this price. In 1958, the last Squariel rolled off the Selly Oak production line. To remain competitive the four would have needed expensive and radical surgery, and the money was needed for a new generation of mould-breaking Ariels, the Leader range of two-stroke twins.

Ariel's Square Four, like the Sunbeam twin produced down the road at Redditch, was another case of 'Nice try, but no cigar'. Both were clever and advanced designs, yet both were fatally flawed. Of the two, perhaps the Ariel best deserves the epithet 'superbike'. It was smooth, effortless and, above all, imposing. It attracted a certain mystique (so much so that a much revised Square Four, the Healy 1000, was produced in limited numbers in the mid-'seventies). Yet in the end, far from liberating British motorcycle manufacturers from the yoke of the vertical twin, it probably deterred them from departing from what they knew best. It is surely the ultimate irony that one man, Edward Turner, was responsible for both.

SPECIFICATION: ARIEL SQUARE FOUR	
ENGINE	air-cooled 997cc OHV square four
HORSEPOWER	42bhp @ 5800rpm
TRANSMISSION	4-speed
FRAME	tubular single loop
BRAKES	drum/drum
TOP SPEED	100mph

Douglas Dragonfly

'In many ways it was a sophisticated yet rugged design.'

The Dragonfly was the final model produced during the chequered and diverse history of the Douglas factory. As well as producing motorcycles, the Kingswood, Bristol company built aero and stationery engines, Vespa scooters, trucks and even dabbled with cars.

Douglas, despite their rather staid reputation, began their days with competition success. Within three years of producing their first motorcycle in 1907, they took the coveted team prize in the International Six Days Trial. Two years later, WH Bashall brought them their first TT win, the 1912 Junior. Such triumphs paved the way to making the company a major manufacturer during World War I, supplying the army with some 70,000 machines.

Further successes followed – first 500cc machine to lap Brooklands at 100mph in 1921; Senior TT victory in 1923 (with a form of disc brake); Sidecar TT laurels the same year. 'Duggies' had become so established that even King George VI acquired one. Whatever else they might offer, 'the best twins' always exuded an aura of class.

Throughout these years, until the end of production in 1957, Douglas championed opposed twin engine layouts, either transverse (like BMW) or, in the early years, fore-and-aft. But the post-war years hit Douglas severely, and in 1948 the receiver was called in, forcing the company to 'rationalise' with a line of models all based on the same 350cc flat twin. At the time, the decision seemed sound. The 1949 'Sports' model was timed at 84mph, allowing Douglas to dub it the world's 'fastest 350 roadster'. But by the time the Dragonfly succeeded the 'Mark' series in 1954, things were very different.

The Dragonfly featured horizontally opposed cylinders and a car-type single plate clutch, but chain final drive. Earles-type Reynolds front forks complemented swing-arm rear suspension, and the novel styling included a headlamp faired into the large petrol tank.

Unmistakably Douglas: smooth, refined and idiosyncratic.

In many ways it was a sophisticated yet rugged design. Cooling was good, the gear cam drive robust, and clutch action uncharacteristically light for the period. Handling and steering was light yet precise, it toured well, and the brakes were good for the time. And, gentlemanly though they were, they also revved, at least in race trim; the last-ever official Douglas TT entry was by a special 90 Plus model in 1954. This spun to 11,000rpm, developed 31bhp, and was timed at 108mph. But, although Duggies had been highly competitive in production-based clubman's racing in the immediate post-war years, by now they had been comprehensively eclipsed. The new clubman's king was BSA's Gold Star.

This was the problem – the Dragonfly was an expensive machine, but it was heavy (365lb), no faster than the MkV it replaced, and failed to satisfy an increasing yearning for performance. Paupers could certainly not afford them, and princes were no longer interested.

At the 1951 Motorcycle Show, Douglas had responded with a 500cc prototype, but even this was not quick and never went into production. However, certain elements – enclosed engine styling, in the manner of BMW, along with a stiffer crankshaft and crankcases and improved lubrication – found a home on the Dragonfly. But, handsome and civilised though it was, the public was unimpressed. Sales were poor, and the Dragonfly was now the only egg in the company's motorcycle basket. Indeed, Douglas' new owners, Westinghouse, seemed more interested in the

Once the choice of kings, but as the horsepower race gathered momentum in the 'fifties, the 350cc boxer became unable to compete with much faster vertical twins.

production of Vespa scooters than the regeneration of the motorcycle range, and by the time motorcycle production ceased in 1957, only 1570 Dragonflies had been built. What was left of the company, Douglas (Sales and Service) Ltd., continued to import and assemble Vespa scooters and later Gilera motorcycles.

SPECIFICATION: DOUGLAS DRAGONFLY

ENGINE	air-cooled OHV 348cc flat twin
HORSEPOWER	17bhp @ 5500rpm
TRANSMISSION	4-speed
FRAME	tubular double cradle
BRAKES	drum/drum
TOP SPEED	72mph

Triumph 650 6T Thunderbird

Triumph's 650 Thunderbird, first launched in 1949, is probably the single machine best known to the post-war generation. For this was the bike ridden so defiantly by Marlon Brando in the 1952 film *The Wild One* ('What are you rebelling against, Johnny?' 'Whaddya got?').

The T-bird also linked two eras. Its engine was the first substantial development of Edward Turner's famous Speed Twin design of 1937 – the machine which was to make parallel twins the mainstay of motorcycle design for over 30 years. Later, even Japan's first attempts at entering the big bike market aped the British layout; Kawasaki's 650cc twin was a near-copy of BSA's A65, although Yamaha's XS1 boasted one overhead camshaft, whilst Honda's CB450 was the first roadster with two.

Yet in pumping out the twin from 500 to 650cc, Turner believed this to be the limit for the design if vibration was not to become excessive. Later 750cc versions (not to mention Norton's 850 Commando), would probably have surprised him. Most riders agree, however, that 650cc was the ideal compromise between smoothness and power.

Although nominally a post-war machine, the T-bird arrived at a time of austerity in Britain, with rationing still in force. The same constraints affected motorcycle manufacturing, although Triumph began the period with a TT victory for Ernie Lyons on a Tiger 100, the sports version of the 500cc Speed Twin. The Thunderbird itself was launched with an impressive publicity stunt. Three machines were ridden to the French race track at Montlhéry, put through 500 laps at an average of

SPECIFICATION: TRIUMPH 650 6T THUNDERBIRD	
ENGINE	air-cooled 649cc parallel twin
HORSEPOWER	34bhp @ 6300rpm
TRANSMISSION	4-speed
FRAME	tubular twin cradle
BRAKES	drum/drum
TOP SPEED	103mph

The Thunderbird — this is a 1956 example — was a response to American demand for more capacity and performance. The result put genuine 'ton-up' potential within reach of the ordinary working man for perhaps the first time.

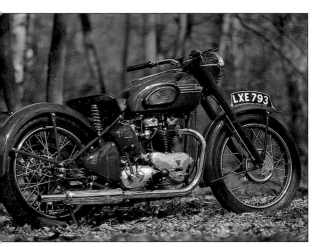

1950 500cc Triumph Speed Twin (far left), precursor of the T'bird. Telescopic forks aside, this is essentially the machine with which Edward Turner launched a generation of British vertical twins.

90mph (with flying laps at over 100mph), then ridden home again. One such machine resides in the Beaulieu motorcycle museum.

In essence the early T-bird was identical to the contemporary Speed Twin, itself substantially a pre-war design, other than the extra 150cc and a change of colour. The air-cooled engine is separate from the gearbox, linked by an enclosed single-row chain. Valve actuation is by push rods from paired camshafts fore and aft of the crankcase mouth.

Rear suspension was by Triumph's ubiquitous sprung hub, for the rear swinging fork had barely arrived. Oil-damped telescopic forks of Triumph design had first replaced girder suspension on the 1946 Speed Twin. Overall, the Thunderbird was a lighter machine than most in its class, with the lively acceleration typical of the marque.

The extra capacity, though, was vital. Consumers, particularly in America, were increasingly demanding more power, and the 650 supplied it in becoming perhaps the first affordable 'ton up' machine. For Triumph, additional costs were modest, and even in the shops the difference between 500 and 650cc was a mere £10, the T-bird costing just £194 when introduced. Other British manufacturers soon followed suit.

When launched, the T-bird was almost in a performance class of its own, and certainly nothing could come near it at the price. In the USA, this frightened Harley-Davidson so much they went to astonishing (but unsuccessful) lengths to thwart Triumph sales. Yet just as the Tiger 100 had evolved as the high-performance version of the Speed Twin, so the need was clear for an even hotter version of the T-bird.

The result was first the Tiger 110 of 1954, then the legendary Bonneville 120, dealt with in a later

It looks sedate now, but in the 'fifties the Triumph's acceleration, handling and brakes were in a different league from Stateside competition, precipitating some underhand tactics from Harley-Davidson.

chapter. Development of the T-bird continued, adding swing-arm rear suspension, light alloy cylinder heads, more power (37bhp by 1960), better brakes and, in 1963, unit construction. By then the controversial 'bathtub' rear bodywork had been largely accepted, as the original concept gave way to a handsome, more civilised touring design. But even 46 years on, the evocative legacy of the Thunderbird name lingers on, in the 900cc triple of born-again Triumph.

'When launched, the T'bird was almost in a performance class of its own.'

Gilera 500-4 Racer

'Part of the machine's continued competitiveness lay in its aerodynamics.'

Gilera, like their Italian competitors MV Agusta, had aristocratic beginnings. In 1909 the Arcore company was founded by Count Giuseppe Gilera, rapidly making its mark as a producer of high-quality singles. But it was for high-revving racing fours that the company is best remembered.

Between the start of the world championship in 1949, and 1957 when they pulled out of racing, Gilera won a remarkable 33 *grands prix*, three manufacturers' championships and six world titles.

The basis for the success was Count Gilera's 1936 acquisition of the Rondine four-cylinder engine, which was itself based on the 1926 OPRA push-rod design. The supercharged Rondine featured double overhead camshafts and liquid cooling. A year later a development of this engine brought Gilera a world speed record of 170mph at the hands of development engineer Piero Taruffi – a success a certain Mr Mussolini was not slow to exploit. In 1939 Dorino Serafini won the 500cc European championship on a similar machine.

Despite inferior handling, the post-war ban on supercharging theoretically favoured Gilera's multi against the opposition singles and twins. Pietro Remor was responsible for redesigning the four into air-cooled, normally-aspirated form. In 1949, two *grand prix* wins brought Nello Pagani and Gilera second place in the inaugural championship. A year later Umberto Masetti went one better, but in 1951 the irrepressible Geoff Duke brought Norton's 500 single their first title. Masetti won again in '52, but for the following year Gilera covered all bases by recruiting Duke to ride the 500. The Englishman took the title in each of the next three years. The 1956 crown went to another British legend, John Surtees, on another Italian four, the MV, before Libero Liberati brought Gilera their last title in

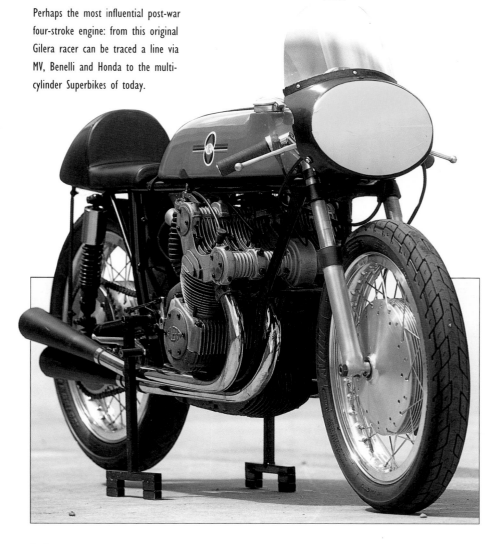

Perhaps the most influential post-war four-stroke engine: from this original Gilera racer can be traced a line via MV, Benelli and Honda to the multi-cylinder Superbikes of today.

1957. In the same year, Bob McIntyre made history when his 500 Gilera became the first machine to lap the Isle of Man TT course at 100mph.

Gilera returned to racing with much the same machinery in 1963, under Duke's *Scuderia Duke* banner. The venture lasted only one season, but it was a measure of the bike's prowess that John Hartle, Phil Read and Derek Minter brought the six year-old hardware to second place in the manufacturers' championship.

Part of the machine's continued competitiveness lay in its aerodynamics. Although the same Pietro Remor was responsible for both engines, the Gilera enjoyed a considerably more compact engine than the MV four, with more efficient and stable streamlining. The Gilera is a mere 15½ inches wide at the crankcases, which split horizontally and contain a built-up roller bearing crankshaft running on six main bearings. The lower left frame rail demounts for engine removal, again permitting a more compact overall design. Each of the cylinder barrels is a separate casting. Its twin overhead camshafts were driven by a central train of gears from the crankshaft.

Although this was a long-stroke design, less revvy and more driveable than later MV and Benelli fours,

its four small cylinders allowed a compression ratio of 11:1 and maximum revs around 11,000. Four 28mm carbs were employed, with four crackling megaphone exhausts at the rear. The Gilera pictured is a 1957 five-speed machine, although an experimental seven-speeder later followed.

Gilera was taken over by Piaggio in 1970, concentrating on small capacity commuter and off-road machines. The early '90s saw an abortive return to 250cc *grand prix* racing. Then, in 1994, the parent company allowed this once great name to die in the name of 'rationalisation'.

As the first of the post-war fours to achieve racing success, the Gilera enjoys a special place in racing history. It would be the Japanese who first put a comparable machine into large scale production, and today the transverse four is by far the most common high-performance format. But it was those fiery Italians who first showed the way.

Remor's masterpiece splits horizontally like later MV-four, with six main bearings carried in magnesium upper crankcase half. The MV was some 1¼ inches wider.

SPECIFICATION: GILERA 500-4 RACER

ENGINE	air-cooled 499cc DOHC four
HORSEPOWER	70bhp @ 10,500rpm
TRANSMISSION	5- or 7-speed
FRAME	tubular steel twin cradle
BRAKES	double drum/drum
TOP SPEED	155mph (over 165mph with dustbin fairing)

Compact Gilera four is astonishingly small, with efficient aerodynamics and a top speed close to 170mph. Weight is around 330lbs.

BMW R69

Of all the 1950s motorcycles in this book, BMW's is the one most readily identifiable today. The Bavarian company has been inextricably associated with horizontally-opposed, shaft-drive twins since Max Friz' original design of 1923. They have equally been associated with high prices and top-quality engineering.

In the late 'fifties, this was almost to prove BMW's downfall. With motorcycle sales plummeting at home, and burdened with the cost of development of a range of small cars, Bee-eM was practically bankrupt. Fortunately the banks bailed them out long enough for the four-wheelers to begin to make their mark – and marks – and the future began to look rosier.

The R69 produced throughout this difficult period was a descendant of the 1951 R67, the company's first 600cc overhead valve twin. Producing 26bhp, the R67 boasted telescopic forks (which, with the 750cc R12 of 1935, BMW had been the first major manufacturer to fit) but rather dated plunger rear suspension.

With the arrival of the R69 in 1955, the teles gave way to pivoted 'Earles-type' front suspension which was then becoming fashionable. At the rear, a new swing-arm set-up was adopted, although at first glance the frame looked like the old plunger trellis. The rebuildable shock absorbers mounted on horns rising up from the main frame rails, which itself swept down close to the rear spindle as before. A rubber sprung saddle mounted airily behind the classic black tank, adding to the dated appearance. A sports version, the R69S, was added in 1960.

Compared to the R67, the 69 had a hotter cam, higher compression pistons, larger carbs and valves, a sports gearbox and nine more horsepower, but was still essentially the same design. Although extremely well-built, with a sturdy pressed-up crank with roller-bearing big-end and main bearings, lubrication is crude and frequent oil-changes essential. The main bearings, which tolerated some whip in the crankshaft, were of a type later to appear as 'Superblend' bearings on later 750cc Norton Commandos. Looked after, the R69 could, like most of its successors, offer prodigious trouble-free mileages.

The R69, with full swing-arm rear suspension and Earles-type forks, was the first 'modern' Beemer twin. Its high price and sheer build quality did much to create BMW's reputation as builders of 'bespoke' motorcycles. This is a 1966 R69S.

Some idea of the painstaking production process is hinted by the availability of cam drive gears in a wide range of sizes to ensure perfect meshing. Not surprisingly, later Bee-eMs adopted chain driven camshafts.

Mechanically, with its heavy cast iron cylinders and needle-roller rockers, the R69 is commendably smooth and quiet. Power, even in 'sport' guise was modest, making the Bee-eM a far more pedestrian machine than contemporary British hot twins. The Earles-type forks, too, were more suited to sidecar than solo use, where they give a vagueness that good teles avoid.

It was, however, a comfortable machine ideally suited to long-distance work on its native autobahns. Despite its weight (445lb ready to roll), it was low and manageable. Above all, it was civilised and, in that uniquely BMW manner, at the same time conservative and defiantly odd. And its price tag was definitely in the superbike league.

As the 'sixties began, the R69 gave way to the /2 twins, which featured detail revisions but were still very much in the same 'fifties mould. Major changes had to wait until 1969 and the R60/5. This, along with its 5-series siblings the 500cc 50/5 and 750cc R75/5, was an altogether more modern-looking machine, with more power, electric start and styling which would last into the eighties. For 1974 the /5 gave way to the five-speed 6 series, now in 600, 750 and 900cc, the latter the 'ultimate' R90S featured on page 84. The last of BMW's 600s was the R60/7 of 1978.

This R60/2 succeeded the 69-series in 1967, but is just as unmistakably BMW. The simple Boxer engine offers a low centre of gravity, shaft final drive and a brand image even Coca-Cola must envy. More Bavarian than *lederhosen*, and probably a great deal more practical.

'It was, however, a comfortable machine ideally suited to long-distance work on its native autobahns.'

SPECIFICATION: BMW R69	
ENGINE	air-cooled 594cc OHV opposed twin
HORSEPOWER	35bhp @ 6800rpm
TRANSMISSION	4-speed, shaft final drive
FRAME	tubular twin cradle
BRAKES	2LS drum/drum
TOP SPEED	102mph

Harley-Davidson Duo-Glide

....

'It didn't much like corners, and was woefully under-braked.'

Few makes of motorcycle arouse such conflicting emotions as Harley-Davidson. To lovers of fast, nimble sports machines in the European tradition, they're slow, heavy and primitive. Others define the same characteristics as laid-back, solid and traditional, and are equally committed to motorcycling as conceived in Milwaukee. As one of the few manufacturers in this book to have been in volume motorcycle production in every one of the 25 years in question, clearly the American way has something going for it.

The Duo-Glide is a case in point. By the time it appeared in 1958, pretty well everything it offered had already been done – and done better – by every other major manufacturer. It didn't much like corners, and was woefully under-braked. But, with its big, slow-revving engine, it was indisputably a Harley. And it was beautiful.

Its roots went back at least to 1922 and the arrival of Harley's first 74 cubic inch (1200cc) Vee-twin model, the 'F-head' JD. In 1930 this became the VL which regressed from inlet-over-exhaust to full side-valve layout – hardly a go-ahead step. Another 11 years produced the Big Twin, now with overhead valves.

In 1948 another engine redesign saw the iron-headed 'Knucklehead' replaced by the 'Panhead', so-called because its rocker covers resembled upturned skillets. The alloy-headed Panhead unit was some eight pounds lighter than before, ran cooler and used hydraulic valve 'lifters' instead of conventional push-rods. Bore and stroke remained the 'traditional' 87 by 101mm (or rather, as Americans still prefer it, $3^7/_{16}$ x 4 inches). 1947 also – whisper it quietly – marked the debut of a range of budget Harley two-strokes that refused to go away for almost 20 years.

However the big event came a year later with the arrival of the first of Milwaukee's 'Glide' models.

Although retaining a rigid rear end, the Hydra-Glide broke with the Harley reliance on leading-link forks. Instead, here was a Hog with a modern telescopic front-end. As if to compensate for this fit of novelty, the Hydra persevered with a uniquely American hand-change gearbox until 1952, and even later as a die-hard option.

The Duo-Glide was the logical next step. As well as real front suspension, the Duo floated on a swinging-arm rear end, hence the name. The hydraulic rear brake was a gimmicky novelty, since both hubs contain tiny six inch single-leading shoe drums which struggle to haul down the 'Glide's substantial bulk.

Harley have always encouraged customising and tuning of their machinery, which invariably comes in a very low state of tune as standard. The example pictured is a 1961 FLH model. The 'H' denotes 'hot' – the engine has an optional high-lift camshaft and higher compression pistons. Even so, power is modest, with a comfortable cruising speed not

SPECIFICATION: HARLEY-DAVIDSON DUO-GLIDE	
ENGINE	air-cooled OHV 1212cc V-twin
HORSEPOWER	54bhp
TRANSMISSION	4-speed
FRAME	tubular steel cradle, single front downtube
BRAKES	drum/drum
TOP SPEED	80mph

much more than 65mph. A 'King of the Road' package includes front and rear nudge bars, twin rear lights and a dual exhaust system.

When Duo-Glide production ceased in 1964, its successor was to become another American legend – the Electra-Glide. The name, and the spirit, endures today. Indeed, current Harley styling, far from modernising the big Vee-twins, has sought to emulate the look of the 'fifties.

Along the way there have been major upheavals. Financial difficulties in the late 'sixties led to an ill-starred merger with AMF, intense competition from Japan, and a disastrous decline in production quality. The 'eighties was to see a management buy-out which initially failed to halt further decline. In the nick of time a new, more reliable range of models, backed by a government tariff on imported models over 700cc, allowed Harley to turn the tide. Today the world's oldest surviving motorcycle manufacturer is in good shape. No other marque is quite like it, and few now command the same passionate loyalty. But for a while, it was touch and go.

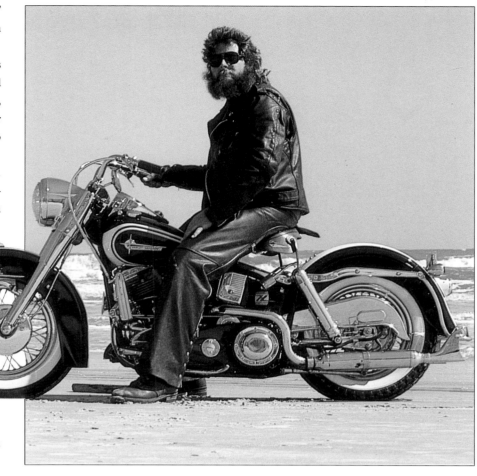

Descended from the Hydra-Glide, the Duo was later to evolve into the quintessential Harley — the Electra-Glide of 1964.

Harleys make a virtue of putting their mechanical parts on display. These days the same classic Milwaukee lines can be seen in 'Retro-tech' machines like the Heritage Softail.

MZ: The Racers

'The only fee
MZ could offer
was the
privilege of
riding one of
the master's
creations.'

Picture shows (left to right) a 1969 liquid-cooled RZ250, 1970 RZ125 tandem twin, 1960 RZ250 and 1960 RE125. During the 'sixties the power of the 125 rose from 22 to 34bhp, while the 250's output climbed from 42 to 58bhp.

Mention the expressions 'MZ' and 'superbike' in the same breath, and the most likely reaction will be incredulous laughter. From its foundation in 1945 until very recently, the former East German company has produced nothing but single-cylinder two-strokes. MZ motorcycles were cheap and cheerful, certainly, but scarcely exotic.

Well yes, and no. MZ roadsters, true, have always been humble machines. But, during the 'fifties and 'sixties, the company produced a range of competition machines that revolutionised two-strokes both on the track and off. Every *grand prix* victory since 1970 (with the exception of MV's swan-song wins), is the legacy of MZ's work.

The company was founded in 1907 by a Dane, Jurgen Rasmussen, initially making parts for textile machinery. In 1915, spurred by wartime petrol shortages, they built a steam-engined car, *Dampf*

Kraft Wagen, which gave the company the name – DKW – it was to carry until the end of World War II. After World War I, the Zschopau-based concern developed a proprietory two-stroke engine, *Das Kleine Wunder* (DKW, again, now meaning 'The Little Marvel').

DKW built its first complete motorcycle in 1922, and by 1928 was using advanced manufacturing methods to build 100,000 units per year, making them the world's largest manufacturer of motorcycles. In 1932 they merged with Audi, Horsch and Wanderer to form Auto Union – a foursome now represented in the four rings worn by Audi motor cars.

DKW soon became prominent in racing, Edwald Kluge bringing them a Lightweight TT victory in 1938. After the war, the rights to the DKW name passed to the West, with a new company, Motorradwerke Zschopau, occupying the old site. For the next 45 years, their principal concern would be to mass produce two-wheelers for the Communist Bloc, with some going for export to earn foreign currency.

There was, however, a competition department – small and under-resourced, but possessing one of the most remarkable minds in the history of motorcycling. When Walter Kaaden took over in 1953, two-strokes had been rendered almost obsolete by the post-war ban on supercharging, on which machines like the pre-war *Ladepumpe* DKWs had depended.

Kaaden's gift to motorcycling was his development of rotary disc induction and tuned expansion chamber exhaust systems, which was to hurl MZ to the forefront of racing development. In 1958, Horst Fügner rode a 250 MZ to the company's first GP win, going on to place second in the world championship. 13 more *grands prix* wins were to follow, a number which would undoubtedly have been far greater had MZ not been so strapped for funds. Ancillary parts for their racing bikes were commonly scrounged or bartered at race meetings.

By 1961, Kaaden had taken the power of MZ's 125cc racer from eight to 25bhp – the first normally-aspirated engine ever to develop 200bhp/litre. These engines, models of elegant simplicity, have since become the building blocks of every successful *grand prix* powerplant of modern times. Indeed, 14 years later the first of Barry Sheene's RG500 Suzukis – unashamedly four

MZ125s in a square box – could boast only 180bhp/litre. In motocross the story is the same.

The early 'sixties, of course, was the time when the Japanese were putting huge sums and effort into *grand prix* racing. And whilst Honda ran four-strokes, Suzuki and Yamaha envied MZ know-how. In 1961, whilst leading the 125cc world championship for MZ, development rider Ernst Degner defected to the West, joining Suzuki. One year later the previously uncompetitive 50cc Suzuki became the first two-stroke to win a world road race championship. Ernst Degner was the rider.

If the impact of Kaaden's work was revolutionary, it was also a triumph for inspired endeavour over the throw-money-at-it approach prevalent elsewhere. Kaaden elevated MZs from paddock curiosities to the fastest racing motorcycles in the world. The MZ riders' list reads like a *Who's Who* of road racing – and all of them did it for nothing, or close to it. The only fee MZ could offer was the privilege of riding one of the master's creations. There were plenty of takers.

1960 MZ RE125, the very machine on which Ernst Degner came so close to winning the 1961 world title, before defecting and handing the crown to Honda (and MZ's technology to Suzuki).

Walter Kaaden (left) photographed in 1993. His genius elevated two-strokes from propelling budget commuter bikes to powering the fastest racing machines in the world.

BSA Gold Star

'Boy racers, after all, will be boys . . .'

The one and only DBD34 'Goldie' was both the ultimate clubmans production racer and *the* single-cylinder street racer of the 'fifties. Yet its origins could not have been more humble, nor more different. For not only was the 500cc Gold Star basically a souped-up B31, but in 1949 it actually began its competitive life on dirt.

The name, of course, was much older. In 1937 the great Wal Handley won at Brooklands on a works-prepared BSA M20 Empire Star, averaging 102.27mph and earning himself a coveted Brooklands gold star medal. Had war not intervened, the Gold Star name was to have been applied to a new sports 500 BSA, the M24 'Handley replica'.

In 1946 the sports mantle passed instead to a tuned version of the unpretentious B31 350cc push-rod single, the B32. In even more highly-tuned form this became the 350cc Gold Star which won the 1949 Clubmans TT at an average speed of over 75mph – on 73-octane 'pool' petrol.

The Gold Star name came from the Brooklands Gold Star awarded for lapping the famed banked circuit at over 100mph. From the very beginning, the Goldie had that sort of pedigree.

The 500cc B34 version arrived in September of the same year, taking no less than eleven gold medals at the ISDT. In 1950 it acquired swing-arm rear suspension, and in a few short years had achieved such utter domination of the Clubmans TT that the races themselves were threatened. The Goldie was becoming too fast for its own good. Of 37 Junior entries in 1955, for instance, no less than 33 were Gold Stars.

But our interest lies with 500cc street versions of what has been described as the 'most anti-social roadster ever made'. The reason for this was simple; the Goldie wasn't really a roadster at all, but a thinly-disguised track machine taking cynical advantage of 'production' racing regulations.

With those compact, elegant lines, the definitive DBD34 Gold Star certainly looks the part. Less apparent is its highly-strung nature, its often temperamental starting and erratic running. With the Amal GP carburettor normally fitted to competition versions, there is little or no drive below 3000rpm, and the high compression engine declines to run at all below 2000. Road versions came equipped with more civilised Amal Monobloc carbs, but didn't always keep them. Boy racers, after all, will be boys . . .

The lack of slow-running is made worse by the Goldie's gearing. The RRT2 competition gearbox was ridiculously tall for street use, necessitating violent clutch slipping from low speed. Silencing was strictly nominal, in either track or street guise, but did produce the Gold Star's famously evocative 'twitter' on the over-run. To appreciate the Goldie you had to take it into its element – if not the race track, then at least the open road. But even the Gold Star's biggest fan would admit that, with its clip-on 'bars and rear-set footrests, it's an uncomfortable machine.

Housing this uncompromising engine was a very ordinary frame almost identical to the 'cooking' B31. This is nonetheless a fairly rigid structure with the quick steering demanded for racing use. The damping, however, is poor and even the Goldie's brakes are nothing special.

What the 500cc Gold Star did have was around 43bhp in race trim, five bhp less for roadsters, both impressive figures for a push-rod two-valve single. This was all the more surprising because the Gold Star's valves were unfashionably small for a performance engine, yet it clearly breathed well.

The secret lay in painstaking detailed refinement of port shapes – and perhaps a little good luck.

Gold Star production ceased in 1962 when BSA declared their highly-strung hooligan single uneconomic to produce. Instead they set about developing a modest 250cc single, the C15, for trials and scrambles. This grew by degrees to 250, 440 and 500cc, gave Jeff Smith two world motocross titles, and transformed off-road sport. From humble beginnings . . .

SPECIFICATION: BSA GOLD STAR	
ENGINE	air-cooled 499cc OHV single
HORSEPOWER	38bhp @ 7000rpm
TRANSMISSION	4-speed
FRAME	tubular double cradle
BRAKES	drum/drum
TOP SPEED	100mph

Elegant yet raw, with no superfluous details, the Goldie was everyone's idea of the classic British single. Although the highly-tuned engine could be a temperamental nightmare, the B31-based chassis proved remarkably able.

Royal Enfield Constellation

....

'Where Triumphs tended to do it on revs, the 'Conny' offered sheer punch.'

Solid and imposing as it was, the Constellation never quite captured the aura enjoyed by Norton and Triumph twins, although a good one was just as fast.

'There is nothing', Americans are fond of saying, 'like cubes'. The US market for both two- and four-wheelers has always had an enduring love affair with cubic capacity for its own sake, a lust that Royal Enfield amongst British motorcycle manufacturers most attempted to satisfy.

Like most other major British factories, Royal Enfield's post war programme was yet another tribute to Alfred Turner's 1937 Triumph Speed Twin design. Royal Enfield saw, as BSA, AMC and Norton also concluded, that their flagship model had to be a four-stroke vertical twin. The layout was compact, relatively easy to manufacturer, fitted readily into a conventional motorcycle chassis and developed a particularly punchy brand of power. So a twin it had to be. But those produced in Redditch would be bigger, and bigger – in America, at least – was best.

Enfield's first post-war vertical twin, the 500cc Meteor, was launched in 1948. This set the pattern for later twins, using a one-piece iron crankshaft, separate heads and barrels, and dry-sump oiling but with the oil neatly held in a reservoir cast integrally with the crankcases. Along with the 350cc Bullet, the Meteor also featured swing-arm rear suspension whilst BSA, Norton and Triumph were still persevering with plunger rear ends.

In the USA, Enfields were sold under the otherwise largely defunct Indian name. Feedback from the States soon prompted the development of a larger machine, and in 1953 the 692cc Meteor was the result (known as the Indian Trailblazer in the US). From the Meteor was derived the Super Meteor, then in 1958 the Constellation – basically a sports version of its predecessor.

692cc was a good deal larger than any other vertical twin on the market. Not surprisingly the

Constellation, and its 736cc successor, the Interceptor, have always been associated with prodigious bottom-end and mid-range power. This is partly due to sheer capacity, partly to the Constellation's long-stroke (70 x 90mm) cylinder dimensions. Where Triumphs tended to do it on revs, the 'Conny' offered sheer punch.

Royal Enfield claimed 51bhp at 6250rpm for the Constellation. At 425lb, weight was relatively modest, and acceleration brisk. In 1960 a Conny was independently timed at 112mph, faster than any other British big twin other than a sports version of the Triumph Bonneville. The down-side ought to have been vibration, to which any such twin is prone, and a big one even more. Enfield substantially reduced this by dynamic balancing of their crankshafts during assembly – the only major manufacturer to do so.

Despite this, Enfield big twins were never so popular as twins from Norton, BSA and Triumph. The engine was regarded as strong, but somewhat staid – often being associated with pulling sidecars, for which it was eminently suited. The gearbox, too – made by Enfield's sister company, Albion – was heavy and slow. Worst of all, they gained a reputation for leaking oil – 'Royal Oilfields' – and for leaky cylinder head joints. Enfield twins also suffered several high-profile breakdowns in major production races. And they simply lacked the cachet enjoyed by many of their rivals.

Constellation production continued until 1962 and the introduction of the 736cc Interceptor, another long-stroke engine with similar characteristics – and shortcomings. A substantially revised Mk2 Interceptor followed, but neither was conspicuously successful and the company sold its last bikes in 1968. Ironically this collapse stranded a shipment of engines en route to Indian in the USA, which subsequently (see page 64) found homes in the Rickman Interceptor. The other Indian connection is that the Enfield name survives in Madras, where 350 and 500cc Bullets continue to be produced.

SPECIFICATION:	ROYAL ENFIELD CONSTELLATION
ENGINE	air-cooled 692cc OHV vertical twin
HORSEPOWER	51bhp @ 6250rpm
TRANSMISSION	4-speed
FRAME	tubular steel cradle, single front downtube
BRAKES	drum/drum
TOP SPEED	112mph

The big Enfields enjoyed dynamically balanced cranks, prodigious torque – and a thoroughly British reputation for leaking oil.

Triumph T120 Bonneville

'Even standing still, it <u>looked</u> 20mph faster than just about any other machine on the road.'

Whatever shortcomings Triumph may have had, struggling to find just the right name for their models wasn't one of them. And if 'Thunderbird' went right to the heart of the American psyche (so much so that Ford later 'borrowed' the name), the legendary Bonneville struck a similar chord.

A development of the Tiger 110, the 'Bonnie' was Triumph's first twin-carb engine since the legendary *Grand Prix* model. The name, of course, came from the famous Bonneville salt flats in Utah, where in 1956 Johnny Allan's streamlined T110 Triumph had clocked the sensational speed of 214mph. The record wasn't accepted by the FIM, but the the reputation stuck – the speed was all that mattered.

For all this pedigree, the T120's start was surprisingly uncertain. The first attempt, in 1959, was a comparatively staid affair, with touring-type mudguards and an ungainly headlamp nacelle. Subsequent versions were altogether leaner and more purposeful-looking. By 1960, even standing still, it *looked* 20mph faster than just about any other machine on the road.

The vertical twin engine produced 46bhp at 6500rpm, fully 12 more than the original Thunderbird. Dry weight was 393lb, 18 more than the T'bird but still light for the class. From the start the Bonnie enjoyed the much stronger one-piece crankshaft introduced in 1959, but other improvements followed year-on-year: twin downtube frame in 1960; unit construction in 1963; 12-volt electrics one year later. Perhaps most important of all was the arrival of Doug Hele at Triumph in 1962. The former Norton man was

Probably the most desirable 'Bonnie' of them all, a 1965 Thruxton model, of which only 64 were built. Distinguished by a heavily tuned engine, competition wheels, brakes and suspension, it took the Bonneville hallmarks of leanness and purpose to their ultimate extremes.

later to find fame as the inspiration behind the success of the 750cc three-cylinder racers, but his first job at Meriden was to improve the geometry and front suspension of Triumph's premier twin.

1962 also saw another shortcoming remedied, at Bonneville itself, when Bill Johnson's Triumph *did* take the speed record on a similar machine at 224.57mph. Two years later Bob Leppan rode another 'Bonnie' streamliner, Gyronaut X-1, to 245.557mph. Although the factory itself was not particularly racing-minded, in 1969 another Bonnie became the first production motorcycle to lap the Isle of Man at 100mph (thus christening Dunlop's TT100 tyre) when Malcolm Uphill took the 'proddy' race with a fastest lap of 100.37mph. Bonnevilles also won the Thruxton 500 mile race, the Le Mans 24-hour races, and many more.

But the Bonnie's real home was on the street, where a 1961 road test described it as 'perhaps the fastest point-to-point roadster produced in Britain today'. Later in the year Triumph offered a carburettor kit offering 117mph, close to the notional '120' of which its name bragged. The

Not Malcolm Uphill, and not a 100mph TT lap, but any biker can dream . . .

T120 was not only the machine to have amongst 'ton-up' kids of the day, but it developed a rare reputation for speed *and* reliability and, at a shade over £284, was actually affordable.

In 1969, and not before time, the Bonnie received the twin leading shoe front brake developed for the new Triumph triples. In 1972 a 52bhp 750cc version, the T140, was added. Yet many riders still consider the 650 the ideal capacity, because vibration made the 750 a painful thing to put through its paces for any length of time.

By now competition from Japanese multis was becoming intense, with the venerable Bonnie increasingly appealing to a niche market. Scarcely had a five-speed T120 been introduced in 1973 than the Triumph/BSA group went bankrupt. With government support, production of Triumph twins eventually passed to the Meriden workers co-operative after a long and rancorous 'sit-in'. 750cc twins, including the £1149 limited edition 'Silver Jubilee' T140V, continued to be built until the collapse of the experiment in 1983. By a matter of months, the Bonnie had failed to reach its own silver jubilee, but the reign had been glorious, all the same.

. . . for if ever a bike awaited the invention of the by-pass to thrash along, the legendary Bonneville was it.

SPECIFICATION: TRIUMPH T120 BONNEVILLE	
ENGINE	air-cooled 649cc parallel twin
HORSEPOWER	46bhp @ 6500rpm (later 51bhp @ 7100rpm)
TRANSMISSION	4-speed (later 120V: 5 speed)
FRAME	tubular twin cradle
BRAKES	drum/drum
TOP SPEED	110mph

Velocette Venom Thruxton

Gaping Amal GP carb gulping unfiltered air did nothing for engine longevity, but for Thruxton owners performance was far more important. Example pictured dates from 1965.

Veloce Ltd., despite occasional and usually blighted adventures with twins, scooters and oddball two strokes, will always be associated with pedigree four-stroke singles. Although a small manufacturer, in the years preceding this book's period they were a potent force in racing – Velocettes took eight Junior TT wins between 1926 and '49, and the inaugural 350cc world championship in 1949, and again when our era began in 1950.

Their road bikes, too, were equally prized – and potent. The company was founded in 1913, and as early as 1921 Velocette were habitual record-breakers with modified roadster machines. Precisely 40 years later they claimed a further fistful of records, included the first 350 to average 100mph for 24 hours (a record which still stands).

From the outset they were an independent-minded company, often producing designs of great technical novelty. But it is singles for which they are best remembered, usually in classy gloss black, picked out with gold pin-striping. Indeed, throughout the 'sixties they made what became the epitome of British road-going singles; the 350cc Viper and 500cc Venom. And most celebrated of all was the 'Thruxton' Venom, the ultimate street-racing single.

This was more than a cosmetic exercise. In 1964 a Venom tricked-out by Reg Orpin of Velocette dealers L Stevens had won the prestigious 500 mile race at Hampshire's Thruxton circuit. From mid-'65 limited numbers of 'replica' Thruxton's were built at the Hall Green factory. Over the next five years, only about 1000 were built, at a retail price of £400 – ten per cent *more* than a Triumph Bonneville twin.

Powering the Thruxton was a hotted-up version of the standard 499cc Venom overhead valve engine. Engine modifications included a 1 3/8 inch Amal GP5 racing carburettor. Special cylinder heads were also used, with huge inlet valves, revised porting, one-piece push-rods and sharper-acting cam-followers.

Before the Thruxton, the Venom Clubman was the hot 500cc Velo. This handsome device is a 1961 model, in more traditional all-black livery.

Equipped with clip-on handlebars, rear-set footrests, a humped seat and long-distance fuel tank, the Thruxton was a factory version of the then-popular 'café racer'. In standard form it wore a Mitchenall full fairing, but many owners dispensed with the lower half, or removed the streamlining altogether.

With or without, it was a wildly impractical machine, demanding considerable mechanical sympathy and a useful touch with the tool kit. Starting any Velocette is tricky, requiring a technique which has become legendary. With 9:1 compression, racing carb and manual-advance magneto ignition, the Thruxton was more pernickety still. Even when running, the 'Thrucky' could be just as contrary. Tuning the engine had made it hesitant at low revs – and the GP5 carb had no idle provision. On later versions an Amal Concentric carb and coil ignition gave better starting and low-speed running.

Maintenance, too, was time-consuming, with the tappets and clutch, in particular, demanding regular attention. Although the engine, with its short, stiff crankshaft, was fundamentally sturdy,

getting it running 'just so' was both a delight and a rarity. But when it did go, it went well, winning the first 500cc Production TT in 1967, at an average speed of 89.89mph. A good Thruxton was capable of 120mph in race tune, well up with the fastest twins.

Even more than its occasional triumphs, the Thruxton attracted the sort of mystique which the motorcycling fraternity reserves for something special. Vincents had it, as Ducatis do today. Velocettes such as this had it in abundance. Sadly others did not. When the company finally went into liquidation on 4 February 1971, what brought them down was the tooling and development costs of, of all things, the Viceroy scooter. Like much that Veloce produced, the little two-stroke twin with reed valve induction was way ahead of its time. But classic machines such as the Thruxton are a far more fitting memorial.

'A good Thruxton was capable of 120mph in race tune.'

SPECIFICATION: VELOCETTE VENOM	
ENGINE	air-cooled 499cc OHV single
HORSEPOWER	41bhp @ 6500rpm
TRANSMISSION	4-speed
FRAME	twin loop with single front downtube
BRAKES	2LS drum/drum
TOP SPEED	120mph (in race trim)

Norton 650SS
....

Designed, like BSA's A10 twin, by Bert Hopwood, the single-camshaft Norton was produced in 500, 600, 650 and later 750 and 850cc form. Of all these the 650SS is the rarest and most desirable.

E ver since their racing exploits of the early 'fifties, Norton were chiefly associated with two things – arguably the best-handling machinery in motorcycling; and the frame which was held responsible, the legendary 'Featherbed'.

In the later 'forties, spurred by the prowess of Alfred Turner's Triumph Speed Twin, Norton (and almost everyone else) sought a twin of their own. Their first design, an in-line twin in the Sunbeam pattern, was rejected as being too unconventional. Jack Moore then drew up a parallel twin, but the model was not built. In 1947 Bert Hopwood arrived and designed what was, in later years, to become Norton's only engine. Not surprisingly, it was similar to the BSA A10 design for which Hopwood was also responsible, but unusual in having a single camshaft across the front of the crankcases. The engine went into production as the 'Dominator' in 1948, but was not available on the home market until late the following year.

Meanwhile the Featherbed frame, designed by the McCandless brothers of Belfast, comprised a bronze-welded duplex cradle with swinging fork rear suspension. Coupled with the 'Roadholder' front forks first introduced in 1948, this conferred an unprecedented level of handling on Norton's racing machines. It first appeared in 1950, replacing the 'Garden Gate' frame on the Manx Norton racer, when its handling was described as 'like a feather bed'. The name stuck.

Although the public was also clamouring for 'proper' rear suspension – and preferably Featherbed frames – their introduction into the Norton range was slow. The problem was that Featherbeds were manufactured for Norton by Reynolds Tubes Ltd., and they could make only 70 per week. So the Featherbed-equipped Dominator 88 de Luxe first shown at Earls Court in 1951, was for export only. As an interim measure, Bob Collier worked out a way of grafting swinging-arm rear ends onto their old lugged frames, which were rushed into the range for 1953.

Eventually the Featherbed became Norton's standard frame, and remained the yardstick by which the handling of other machinery was judged long after production ceased in the late 'sixties. Indeed the Japanese were to imitate the design for a further 20 years. But in the 'fifties, if Norton had a problem, it was in developing an engine worthy of the Roadholder/Featherbed package.

In late 1955 the 600cc Dominator 99 was added to its 500cc stablemate. The bigger engine was, like all subsequent Nortons, non-unit (a Hopwood-led unit-construction project begun in the late 'fifties was later abandoned). It developed 31bhp at 5750rpm – an improvement, but significantly less than Triumph's sporting twin. In 1960 a revised Featherbed, the 'Slimline' was introduced. Then, in 1961, came the 650SS, initially for export only.

With comparable products already available from BSA, Royal Enfield, AJS/Matchless and Triumph (the Bonneville first appeared in '59), the SS had to be good – and it was. Early versions suffered some failures – notably burst cylinder barrels and fatigue fractures of various fittings – but through it all shone that pedigree handling package. Ridden to the limit, no other production machine could come close. And with a top speed comfortably over 110mph, the new Norton was no slouch on the straights. Not surprisingly, the 650SS went on to win production races by the score.

Yet for all this success, these were troubled times for Norton. In 1962 they amalgamated with the AMC Group. The 750cc Norton Atlas appeared on the home market two years later, the same engine appearing as the Matchless G15 under the AMC flag. Four years later still, the 650SS was succeeded by the single-carburettor Mercury, and in the same year AMC themselves collapsed into liquidation. Norton Villiers arose from that

particular pile of ashes, and with them, the next generation of Norton vertical twins – the Commando.

On any half-interesting road, all you'd see of a well-ridden SS was this badge disappearing into the distance.

SPECIFICATION: NORTON 650SS	
ENGINE	air-cooled 647cc OHV vertical twin
HORSEPOWER	49bhp @ 6800rpm
TRANSMISSION	4-speed
FRAME	'Featherbed' duplex steel cradle
BRAKES	drum/drum
TOP SPEED	115mph

'Ridden to the limit, no other production machine could come close.'

The 650SS added serious horsepower to the already 'unapproachable' Norton chassis. Almost out of the crate, the newcomer was capable of winning races.

Honda RC165 250-6 Racer

....

'With Hailwood on board, the six began to fly.'

By any standards the Honda story is remarkable. From the time Soichiro Honda sold his first motorcycle in 1948, it was to be barely 20 years before his dream of providing motorcycles for the masses established his company as the world's largest producer of two-wheelers. This explosive growth was built on a rush of technology which was equally staggering. And in the minds of the motorcycling public no machine epitomised it quite so vividly as the six-cylinder 250cc racer.

The year was 1964, just five short years after Honda's debut at the Isle of Man TT. Yet by 1961 Honda had taken their first world championship crown, two times over – Mike Hailwood taking the 250cc title, Rob Phillis the 125.

Although Honda went on to become the dominant force in 125, 250 and 350cc *grands prix*, their Japanese rivals were also making spectacular progress with two-strokes of ever-increasing power and complexity. Of this 'new wave', only Honda were committed to four-stroke engines, and the two-strokes were intrinsically more powerful.

When Phil Read handed Yamaha the prized 250cc title in 1964 and again in 1965, Honda had to do something dramatic. The result, in this crazy, helter-skelter decade, was

Never has so much technology been packed into a mere quarter litre. Six cylinders, six carbs, 24 valves and 18,000rpm made the 250-6 perhaps the most sensational device in the history of *grands prix*.

the unforgettable 250-6 taken by Soichiro Irimajiri's design team from drawing board to prototype in just two months. Although debuted by Jim Redman in a desperate attempt to stem the Yamaha challenge at Monza late in 1964, the six's first full season was a disappointment. Handling and reliability problems, and Redman's loss of form, handed the '65 title to an irrepressible Read. Then, at the last *grand prix* of the season, the Japanese, one of racing's great partnerships began: Hailwood, still riding MVs in the larger classes, climbed aboard the Honda six.

Hailwood won, but his outspoken criticism of the machine's handling caused headlines in a country more accustomed to dignified restraint. Yet when Honda signed him for the 1966 season, they gained not only his unparalleled riding ability, but his diagnostic experience as well. With Hailwood on board, the six began to fly, winning no less than ten of the 12 *grands prix*. For good measure he took the 350cc world title with a 297cc machine, the RC174, which was essentially a bored and stroked 250-six.

For Honda nothing less would have done, for this was the season in which they attempted an unprecedented piece of audacity; to win all five solo

championship classes. They were partly successful, in that they took the manufacturers' title in each, but provided champions in 'only' three – Agostini took the 500 title for MV, Anscheidt winning on the 50cc Suzuki. In all, Honda scored 29 *grands prix* wins in this single season.

The rationale for the six was that if a four-stroke was to compete with the strokers, it had to compensate for having only half as many firing strokes by breathing better and spinning faster. This meant smaller cylinders with a very short stroke and, inevitably, lots of them. The 250's cylinders were just 39mm across, with a stroke of 34.5mm. It meant four valves per cylinder – 24 in all – and double overhead camshafts. It meant no less than six 17mm flat-slide Keihin carburettors. Most of all, it meant revs; the six eventually produced its peak power of 60bhp at a giddy 18,000rpm (the even more outrageous 125-five revved well beyond 19,000rpm).

Placing six cylinders in-line across the frame was not the obvious choice, yet this miracle of miniaturisation was no wider across the fairing than a contemporary racing single. The 150mph machine weighed just 260lbs.

In 1967, Honda pulled out of *grand prix* racing. But no-one who saw – or heard – the six will ever forget it.

A masterpiece of miniaturisation, the 250's six cylinders – count 'em – made it no wider across the fairing than many a single.

SPECIFICATION: HONDA RC165 250-6 RACER	
ENGINE	air-cooled 247cc DOHC transverse six
HORSEPOWER	60bhp @ 18,000rpm
TRANSMISSION	7-speed
FRAME	tubular steel open cradle
BRAKES	double drum/drum
TOP SPEED	153mph

Suzuki T20 'Super Six'

....

This was the machine that first put the writing on the wall for the British motorcycle industry. In 1966, when Suzuki's 'Super Six' was introduced, multi-cylindered Oriental behemoths were still but a distant dream. Yet if Honda's CB750 was to be dubbed the first 'superbike', the little Suzuki was the first roadster to reveal the awesome potential of the emerging Japanese giants.

During its first six months on sale, over a thousand Super Sixes were sold in the UK alone. More ominously still, in December 1966 it became the first Oriental motorcycle to be voted 'Machine of the Year' by readers of *MotorCycle News*. One year later it retained the title.

The attraction, of course, lay in the numbers. The 'six' that were 'super' were gears, an unprecedented number for a roadster. (They were also an insult – two years previously, Royal Enfield's first five-speed 250 sports bike was named the

Super Five.) Then there was 100, the top speed alleged in T20 marketing hype. The Super Six was capable of nothing like that in neutral conditions, of course. But even a genuine 90mph was enough to shame many a 500, and thoroughly see off any European 250 foolish enough to give chase.

Also unprecedented was the Suzuki's level of technical sophistication, detailing and reliability – in a truly sporting package at an affordable price. When introduced, the machine cost less than £2 more than the comparable, but much slower, Enfield Continental GT.

To fully appreciate a Super Six, however, you need to strip it. Invert the engine, lift off the bottom crankcase half (the cases split horizontally, unlike Suzuki's previous 250, the T10) and a design of surpassing elegance lies before you.

There are three main shafts – crank-, lay- and mainshaft, with a final train of gears driving the Suzuki's novel Posi-Force oil pump (which

Suzuki's T20 set the world back on it heels in producing 500cc performance from such a tiny package. Inside, the engine was even more impressive.

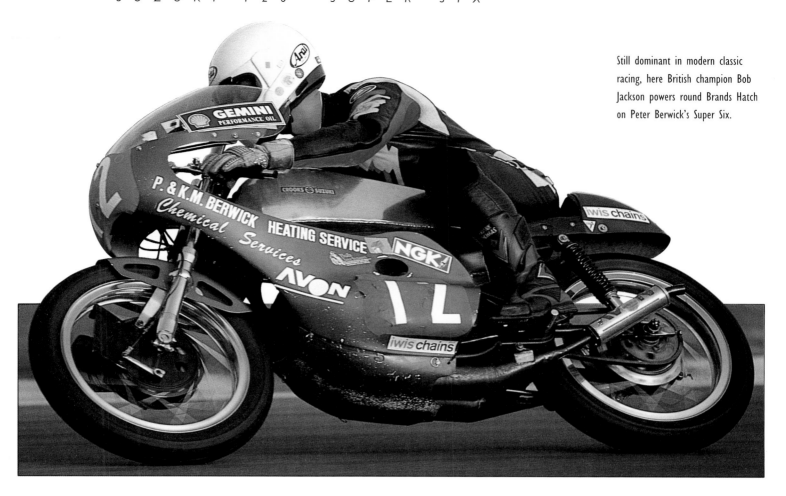

Still dominant in modern classic racing, here British champion Bob Jackson powers round Brands Hatch on Peter Berwick's Super Six.

dispensed with the messy job of mixing oil and fuel). The crank runs on three main bearings, the outer two being lubricated directly by the oil pump, the centre one by gearbox oil. One-piece steel connecting rods run on the pressed-up crank, their roller big-ends receiving oil from the outer mains. Small ends are needle roller, supporting cast, two-ring pistons with a shallow dome. Primary drive is by gear.

Each cylinder has its own head and iron-sleeved barrel, the latter sporting 'classic' 54x54mm dimensions. Porting was conservative by modern standards, with the inlet port bridged to give the piston rings an easier life. It was an exquisite, seminal design, barely distinguishable in principle from racing Yamahas of 20 years later. It was light (297lb), reliable, and started easily. But most of all – although the claimed 29bhp is optimistic – it was fast.

The T20 was regarded in its time as a good handler, with damping 'superior to any [other] Japanese machine'. In truth, the suspension was harsh, and the brakes no better than adequate. It has a general air of flimsiness which was largely overcome with the introduction of the much sturdier T250 Hustler in 1969.

Not surprisingly Super Sixes found their way onto the tracks in large numbers, both in standard guise and as the 'kitted' TR250. On a good day the TR250 was a match for Yamaha's contemporary TD1C. As well as race wins – notably in the '67 Manx Grand Prix – modified Eddie Crooks T20s broke world records over six hours, 1000km, 12 hours and 24 hours (the latter in 256cc '350' form, at 91.055mph). They were even modified for off-road competition.

Thirty years on, the Super Six inevitably feels dated. Its power is around half that of a modern sports 250, and the chassis and cycle parts come from a different planet. Yet despite that, it was a revelation in its day and has an unmistakable feel of modern-ness about it. And, above all, it set in train a revolution that is still winning races today. With the Super Six, less truly was more.

SPECIFICATION: SUZUKI T20 'SUPER SIX'	
ENGINE	247cc two-stroke parallel twin
HORSEPOWER	29bhp @ 7500rpm
TRANSMISSION	6-speed
FRAME	tubular double cradle
BRAKES	drum/drum
TOP SPEED	90mph

'It was an exquisite, seminal design, barely distinguishable from racing Yamahas of 20 years later.'

Honda CB450 'Black Bomber'

....

'Despite its chequered history, the Bomber was undoubtedly a major breakthrough.'

In 1965, a large-capacity Japanese vertical twin represented a frontal attack on the entire British motorcycle industry. The advanced but flawed CB450 failed to win the battle, but Honda unquestionably won the war.

Although Honda's CB750-four was the more awe-inspiring machine, the CB450 twin introduced in 1965 was in many ways more technologically advanced. Perhaps more crucially still, it was also the bike the British motorcycle industry deluded themselves into thinking Japan couldn't build; a large capacity, high performance four-stroke. The CB450 put the writing graphically on the wall.

By the time the 'Black Bomber' arrived, Honda four-stroke roadsters were already achieving remarkable speeds and healthy sales in the smaller classes. The largest previous model was the 305cc CB77, a sports twin derived from the 250cc CB72, and capable of over 95mph. Yet both Soichiro Honda's technology-driven philosophy of constant development, and the aspirations of marketing chief, Fujisawa, demanded more. The result, ready to cash in on the American preoccupation with large-capacity machines, was the CB450.

Although the vertical twin engine layout was conservative, the Bomber's internals were not. Rather than follow the British practice whereby the pistons rise and fall together, the CB450 featured crank throws 180 degrees out of phase, substantially reducing primary imbalance and vibration.

Instead of conventional coil springs, the Honda's valves were closed by torsion bars. But most dramatic of all was the use of twin overhead camshafts, a system previously confined to exotic racing machines. Bore and stroke were substantially oversquare at 70 x 57.8mm, allowing the engine to fully exploit the valvegear's capacity for revs. An electric starter was also fitted.

The result was a motorcycle that was not only as civilised and convenient as its Japanese predecessors, but as fast as many a British 650. Early versions, finished in black and chrome (hence the affectionate 'Black Bomber' tag) produced 43bhp.

Sales of the CB450 were quite good in the UK, but not where it counted; the USA. For Honda's first large capacity machine turned out to be as flawed as it was innovative. Maintenance, especially valve-lash adjustment, was laborious. Cylinder head removal required the splitting and re-rivetting of the cam chain. The handling, particularly at low speed, was peculiar. And the original tyres did more to protect the rims than offer grip.

Perhaps worst of all, the Bomber wasn't notably reliable, and it *did* vibrate. The uneven firing intervals of 180 degree crank manifested themselves in snatchy low-speed running which the relatively small flywheels were unable to overcome. This was made all the more intrusive by the widely-spaced ratios of a gearbox with just four speeds. At high revs, however, it was uncannily smooth for a parallel twin.

In 1967 an improved model was developed, with five speeds, different carburettors, a claimed 45bhp, and a top speed of around 104mph. Chassis modifications also improved the handling, but the die had been cast; the CB450 was not the success that Honda had hoped for.

Despite its chequered history, the Bomber was undoubtedly a major breakthrough. A double overhead camshaft engine had previously been considered far too expensive to produce for an ordinary roadster, yet Honda managed to build one, ship it halfway around the world, and still make a handsome profit. Their solution was to use a simple, single roller-less chain where expensive spur-gears or bevels were conventionally used. Such chains were cheap, and dispensing with rollers eliminated the possibility of one breaking and wrecking the engine. The inherent noise of the system was reduced by cunning use of guides, rollers and quietening rubbers.

However, novelty has a price. The first batch of Bombers were embarrassingly recalled due to top-end wear – caused by rubber quietening inserts in the timing gear breaking up and finding their way into the oil pump. More dramatic still was a tendency for a cam chain idler gear to fall into the crankcases, and the early constant velocity carburettors' habit of sticking wide open.

Yet the CB450 set a trend: almost every overhead camshaft Honda motorcycle engine produced since has employed a broadly similar set-up. Whilst it must be said that Honda have sometimes got their cam-drives embarrassingly wrong, the CB450 set them along the right path.

Before the CB450, twin overhead camshafts had been the exclusive preserve of exotic factory racers.

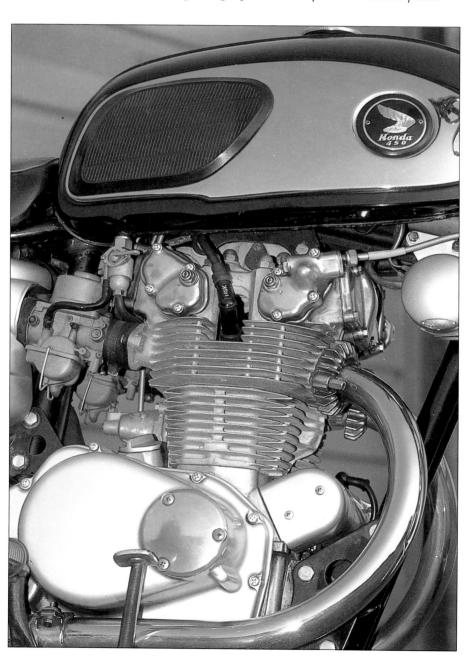

SPECIFICATION: HONDA CB450 'BLACK BOMBER'	
ENGINE	air-cooled 444cc DOHC vertical twin
HORSEPOWER	43-45bhp @ 9000rpm
TRANSMISSION	4-speed (later 5-speed)
FRAME	tubular steel single cradle
BRAKES	drum/drum
TOP SPEED	104mph

Bridgestone 350 GTR

....

'The GTR was also the smoothest in its class.'

Bridgestone's foray into motorcycle production was brief, but memorable. With disc-valve induction, six speeds, chrome bores and a 'piggy-back' alternator, the GTR anticipated many of the advances of the following decade.

If Suzuki's Super Six was the people's two-stroke screamer back in the late 'sixties, the 350GTR was the connoisseur's. Never had any stroker featured such a level of specification, not to mention acceleration capable of humbling many a 650 twin.

Bridgestone began making motorcycles in 1952, the same year Suzuki's production began. Although the GTR was essentially similar in design to the Super Six which had appeared a year earlier, it was awash with even more advanced touches. Like the Suzuki (and contemporary Yamahas and Kawasakis), the Bridgestone's crankcases split horizontally to reveal crank-, lay- and main-shafts laid out neatly for inspection. Also like the Suzuki, it featured six-speed transmission.

Where the GTR differed most was in its use of disc valve induction. A 'normal' two-stroke uses the rise and fall of the piston to control the flow of incoming and exhaust gases through ports in the cylinder walls. Because this inevitably gives symmetrical port timing, it can lead to poor running and spitting back through the carb, particularly at lower revs.

By offering asymmetric timing, rotary disc valves – basically cutaway discs mounted on the crankshaft – can overcome this problem. The system was perfected by MZ's race engineer, Walter Kaaden, before the technology was stolen – by Suzuki – in 1961. The Bridgestone wears two such disc valves – one per cylinder – keyed to each end of the crankshaft. A 26mm Mikuni carb sits outboard of each of these.

There was more. Since the side-mounted carbs make the powerplant quite broad enough, a 'piggy-back' alternator kept engine width within acceptable limits. The cylinder bores, rather than being of iron, are hard chrome, allowing tighter piston clearances. A dry, racing-style clutch is fitted. Not new, but welcome, is 'Jet Lube' positive oiling (driven by a pump under the right-hand carb), a version of the system first introduced on Yamaha's 1964 YA6. The 2.5 litre oil tank features an inspection window, with another allowing riders to check gearbox oil level; both commonplace later, but huge refinements at the time.

In the 'sixties, of course, half the world was changing gear with its right foot, the other half with its left. The GTR accommodated both; gearchange and rear brake pedals could be swapped. Less intelligent was the positioning of neutral above sixth gear in the down-for-up gearbox. Another 'modern' touch was that the 350 could be kick-started in gear, although the left-side kick start was rather less convenient.

More fashionable were the inflated performance claims made for the GTR – anything between 100 and 110mph. The reality, despite a speedo calibrated to 140, was around 93mph. In 1967 this nonetheless made the bike probably the quickest two-stroke roadster ever built.

Thanks to its rubber-mounted engine, the GTR was also the smoothest in its class. 37bhp (40bhp

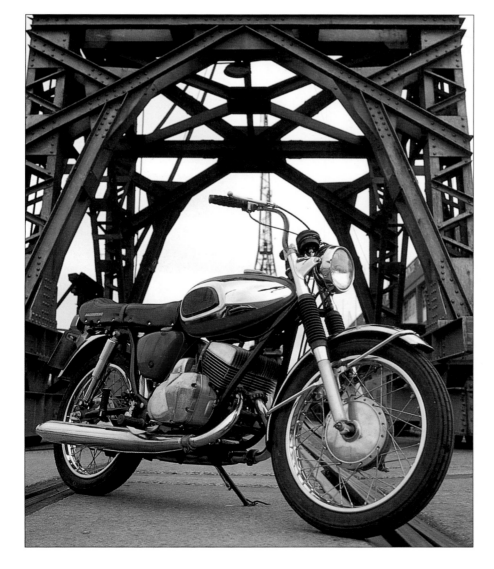

was also claimed) offered searing acceleration with that exhilarating rush typical of performance two-strokes. The 330lb machine handled well on suspension that was more supple than most, and the drum brakes were equally impressive.

Not only was this specification impressive, but the build quality of the Bridgestone was also exceptional. Unfortunately, so, too, was the price. In 1968 a GTR retailed at £340, about £60 more than a Super Six and only £29 less than a Triumph 650 Bonneville. This, and widespread doubts about the durability of such 'buzz boxes', severely restricted sales. Just 33 GTRs were imported to the UK before Bridgestone abruptly ceased motorcycle production in late 1968 to concentrate on its core tyre-making business. The 350 GTR may not have lasted long, but it was certainly memorable.

Advanced disc-valve induction (above right) put the Bridgestone one jump ahead. Like other Japanese machines of the period, the GTR's engine was way ahead of its chassis.

SPECIFICATION: BRIDGESTONE 350 GTR	
ENGINE	air-cooled 345cc disc-valve two-stroke twin
HORSEPOWER	37bhp @ 7500rpm
TRANSMISSION	6-speed
FRAME	tubular double cradle
BRAKES	2LS drum/drum
TOP SPEED	93mph

Suzuki RS67 Racer

·····························

This is a tale of a headlong technological onslaught such as we may never see again. If Europeans were inclined to laugh at Japan's early forays into *grand prix* racing, it was Suzuki who gave them the most opportunities. When Suzuki entered the world championship in 1960, the unreliability of their machinery was only equalled by its slowness. Their 125, for instance, developed a mere 13bhp, substantially less than Honda's RC142 and about *ten horsepower* fewer than Ernst Degner's East German MZ RE125.

Even in 1961, when Honda were winning their first TT, the Suzukis were woefully uncompetitive. Yet just 12 months later a 50cc Suzuki became the first two-stroke ever to win a world championship. A year later still, Hugh Anderson gave Suzuki their first 125cc world title. Suzuki had arrived.

The difference was largely due to one man; that same Ernst Degner, who had defected to the West

in 1961 whilst leading the 125cc championship. His escape was 'sponsored' by Suzuki, for whom Degner was soon working under an assumed name. At the time, thanks to the genius of Walter Kaaden, MZ were masters of the two-stroke technology to which Suzuki aspired. Degner was the means of obtaining it.

For the most part, it worked. But, such was Anderson's success that Suzuki grew bold. For 1964, they decided to aim for the 250cc title as well. The result, the RZ64 liquid-cooled 'double 125' square four, has been described as 'one of the most embarrassing flops in *grand prix* history'. In two years of GP racing, it never finished higher than third. Even to this day, Suzuki has never won a 250c world road race title.

Although Suzuki continued to win the 50cc title, the major titles eluded them other than Anderson's repeat 125cc win in 1965. Honda had leap-frogged

Despite a lightweight aluminium frame, the RS67's chassis parts were primitive. What mattered most was cramming maximum technology into minimum volume, at which the V4 excelled. Sadly, Suzuki withdrew from racing before it was fully developed.

to the 1964 125cc championship with an eight-speed transverse four. In 1966 they responded just as emphatically with their miraculous 125cc-five, effectively 2½ 50cc twins. Thus equipped, Taveri won again, although harried all the way by Bill Ivy's V4 Yamaha.

Against this relentless development, when even the most sophisticated machine could be rendered obsolete in less than 12 months, Suzuki needed something far more potent than the ageing 35bhp RT67 twin with which they contested most of the 1967 series. After just four frantic months of development the V4 was ready to race at the last *grand prix* of the year, the Japanese, in October.

The RS67 is a still-incredible machine which must have been mind-blowing at the time; four tiny cylinders in 90 degree vee formation, four 24mm carbs, four geared cranks, 12 gears, liquid-cooled, with positive oil lubrication and disc-valve induction.

Peak power was 42bhp – over *three times* greater than Suzuki's 125 of a mere seven years earlier – at a dizzy 16,500rpm. Top speed was 136mph. To

reduce friction losses, the gearbox was dry-sump, with forced lubrication from a trochoidal pump. Yet for all this complexity, extensive use of titanium and aluminium alloys (even the frame was aluminium), kept weight down to just 95kg – only 6kg more than the twin.

When Stuart Graham placed second to Bill Ivy at the Fuji circuit, the signs were encouraging. Yamaha may have taken the championship, but the new Suzuki was clearly a force to be reckoned with. By February 1968, power had improved to 43.8bhp. Suzuki were also developing the astonishing RP68, a 50cc Vee-3 which reportedly produced 19.8bhp at 19,000rpm – the highest specific output ever recorded by a normally-aspirated internal combustion engine. It was so peaky that its 14 gears were insufficient.

Yet time was running out for the multi-cylinder factory specials. 125s were soon to be limited to two cylinders and six speeds. When Suzuki, along with Honda, withdrew from world championship competition, the days of the most exotic generation of machines in racing history were over.

The product of Japanese engineering enterprise and East German genius, the V4's disc valves and screaming expansion chambers produced an astonishing 340bhp/litre.

SPECIFICATION: SUZUKI RS67 RACER	
ENGINE	liquid-cooled 124cc two-stroke V4
HORSEPOWER	42bhp @ 16,500rpm
TRANSMISSION	12-speed
FRAME	aluminium twin cradle
BRAKES	drum/drum
TOP SPEED	136mph

'The new Suzuki was clearly a force to be reckoned with.'

BSA Spitfire

They didn't know it at the time, but when the Spitfire arrived, BSA had a distinctly chequered future.

Understated but potent, the Spitfire was too little, too late to reverse the decline in BSA's fortunes. By the time the MkIV arrived in 1968, Honda's CB750 was just around the corner.

BSA's first post-war big twin, the 500cc Model A7, first came under public gaze at the Paris Motorcycle Show of 1946. Public reaction was favourable, but the bike's wasn't: performance proved to be disappointing, with a tendency to 'run-on' through self-ignition.

Cue Bert Hopwood, one of the most creative spirits in post-war British motorcycle design and the man also responsible for Norton's enduring Dominator. These days he might easily be described as 'Twins-R-Us'. Hopwood redesigned the 500cc BSA twin into the 650cc A10 Golden Flash. This in turn generated a better A7, plus a sports 500 known as the Star Twin.

In 1952 the Star Twin made one of the most impressive attempts on the Maudes Trophy, awarded for feats of exceptional motorcycle endurance. Three Star Twins were ridden 1000 miles to the ISDT in Austria, competed (earning gold medals apiece), then continued until each machine had completed 4900 miles. Not surprisingly, this earned BSA the coveted trophy, and a reputation for mechanical strength.

The unit construction BSA A50/A65 series followed early in 1962, prompted by Triumph's similar move. As well as eliminating the primary chain adjustment, the new twins had better electrics, weighed some 30lbs less than their predecessors, and were significantly less expensive than their Triumph competitors. They had clean, neat lines – perhaps too neat, because many considered the styling bland. But the first A65 claimed only 38bhp, and there was soon some concern about main bearing and oil pump failures. For whatever reason, the public wasn't impressed.

The performance benchmark during the early 'sixties was of course Triumph's T120 Bonneville, whilst Norton set the yardstick for handling. BSA twins, on the other hand, were ideal sidecar hacks with a reputation for robustness rather than sparkling looks or performance.

True, BSA had created some worthy contenders, notably the A10RGS Rocket Gold Star twin. But these were specialised machines produced in relatively small numbers. It wasn't until the arrival of the Spitfire in 1965 that BSA truly entered the fray (British bikers had to wait until 1966). Although basically a development of the twin-carb A65L Lightning, this was a much more single-minded beast. With vibrant red paintwork, alloy wheel rims, close-ratio gears, high-compression pistons and substantially less weight, this was the Beezer they'd been waiting for.

The first Spitfire, with racing-style Amal GP carburettors and hot camshafts, claimed a potent 55bhp. Later examples were slightly de-tuned, if less raucous, with Concentric carbs and slightly less compression. The chassis, on the other hand, was only slightly different from 'cooking' BSA twins. And, worst of all, the short-stroke twin vibrated savagely at high revs.

1968 brought the last of the Spitfires, the MkIV, with a twin leading shoe front brake and audacious 150mph speedometer. More pointedly still, it brought the first public showing for Honda's CB750. BSA actually did the right thing in buying a Honda four for evaluation. Astonishingly, when its chain snapped after less than 100 miles and wrecked the crankcases, they felt able to dismiss the growing hurricane from the East as an inconsequential breeze.

Although a revised range of twins with oil-bearing frames appeared in 1970, these were unattractively styled and increasingly dated in overall design. Ironically, during this period BSA boasted a highly sophisticated development department at 'space age' Umberslade Hall, and perhaps the most automated motorcycle production line outside Japan. Yet for all this potential the company flapped around like a headless chicken, producing a succession of misbegotten models in search of a replacement for the venerable Bantam. These included the Dandy and Beagle commuter bikes, a 250cc scooter and the catastrophic Ariel-3 tricycle. Perhaps the most promising project, the 350cc ohc Fury twin, never reached production. In 1973, this one-time giant gently subsided, its remaining assets passing to the Norton-Villiers group.

This particular MkIV Spitfire is still going strong despatch riding around London. The Spit's always-considerable punch has been made even stronger by a 834cc top-end, although the brakes struggle to cope with modern traffic conditions.

SPECIFICATION: BSA SPITFIRE	
ENGINE	air-cooled 654cc OHV vertical twin
HORSEPOWER	up to 55bhp @ 7000rpm
TRANSMISSION	4-speed
FRAME	tubular steel twin cradle
BRAKES	drum/drum
TOP SPEED	110mph

'This was a much more single-minded beast.'

Triumph Trident 750

For once, advertising told the truth. When the BSA/Triumph triple was launched in 1968, the advertising insisted that 'After today, the motorcycle world will never be the same'. It wasn't, but it was Honda, rather than BSA/Triumph, who prospered. The triple was in some ways a better machine than the shattering CB750 launched one year later. It certainly handled far better, yet somehow it never quite cut it against the sophistication and sheer flamboyance of the four.

Originally the BSA Group (which had acquired Triumph/Ariel in 1951) produced two versions, the Triumph Trident T150 and the BSA Rocket-3. The latter used forward-inclined cylinders in a tubular twin cradle, compared to the Triumph's upright powerplant in a single-downtube 650-type frame.

But the powerplant, imposing as it was, was little more than a stop-gap measure, proposed by two of the rare forward-thinkers in the British industry at the time. Designers Bert Hopwood and Doug Hele had proposed such an engine, essentially 1 1/2 Triumph Tigers on a common crankcase, some years earlier. In the longer term Hopwood favoured a modular engine system, not unlike that adopted by the Bloor/Triumph company 20 years later.

In the meantime, the Trident would have to suffice against the multis known to be coming from Japan, and it did so pretty well. A good one was at least as fast as the Honda (the first press test Trident, possibly a 'special', clocked almost 130mph; others struggled to reach 118mph). The handling, though good, was undoubtedly

Virtually 1 1/2 500cc Triumph twins on a common crankcase, the triple wasn't quite sophisticated enough to exploit the multi-cylinder era it anticipated.

'The handling, though good, was undoubtedly compromised by the sheer mass of the beast.'

Although now much sought-after, the striking Craig Vetter-designed X-75 Hurricane version of the triple (below and left) was not the sales success BSA/Triumph hoped. If only the same flair had been allowed in R&D . . .

compromised by the sheer mass of the beast. Nonetheless, it could leave the Honda for dead through the turns.

Mechanically, though, this was the triple that Edward Turner might have designed in 1937. Pushrods opened the valves, at a time when overhead camshafts were becoming commonplace. The crankcases split vertically, like the twin's, and primary drive was by chain. A diaphragm clutch was more up-to-date, but the original four-speed gearbox was not. Overall, despite Ogle Design's styling of the BSA (with 'Ray-gun' silencers and 'Bread-bin' fuel tank), the bike was more a child of the 'sixties than the imminent 'seventies.

Where the triple scored its biggest success was on the track, where anyone who heard it still shivers from that haunting wail. For British race fans of the 'seventies, the Rob North-framed triple was the 'feel-good' factor on two wheels – first, second and third at Daytona in 1971; countless other short-circuit victories, and a succession of production TT wins for the legendary 'Slippery Sam'.

On early versions the equipment, too, was less than state-of-the-art. Triumph's twin leading shoe drum front brake was never very potent; on the 460lb triple it was downright embarrassing. Starting, unlike the Honda's, was by kick.

(Ironically, BSA bought an early CB750 for evaluation. When its drive chain broke after less than 100 miles, they dismissed the entire machine as 'no threat'). Despite a higher selling price, it simply wasn't as refined as the Honda.

When it finally arrived, the Triumph-Lockheed disc front brake was good, but by then the triple had been five years in production. Also in 1973, attempts to improve sales resulted in the X-75 Hurricane, one of the most eye-catching roadsters ever produced; it flopped. Two years later still the Triumph T160 electric start version appeared, now with more power from an engine leaning forward in the old Rocket-3 manner.

It was all too little, and too late. In 1973 the bankrupt BSA Group amalgamated with Norton-Villiers, planning closure of the Triumph factory at Meriden. This provoked the famous workers' sit-in which, after the election of a Labour government in February 1974, established Meriden as an independent cooperative. Henceforth, however, it would produce only twins.

SPECIFICATION: TRIUMPH TRIDENT 750	
ENGINE	air-cooled 740cc OHV transverse triple
HORSEPOWER	58bhp @ 7500rpm
TRANSMISSION	5-speed
FRAME	tubular twin cradle with single front downtube
BRAKES	2LS drum/drum (1972-on: disc/drum)
TOP SPEED	120mph

Honda CB750

....

'Fastidious little cable guides abound, and the instruments are elegant in their one-piece neatness.'

Prior to 1969, the word 'Superbike' simply didn't exist. Then Honda's seminal 750-four came along, opening up a whole new lexicon of jargon, and a revolution in motorcycle design. Almost every Japanese superbike – and many not so super – can trace its ancestry back to this one machine.

Honda's *coup* – even more than winning Daytona with the four in 1970 – was in putting such a device into mass production. Engine technology, far from being at the cutting edge, was fairly old hat. Honda already made twin-cam roadsters (CB450), but the 750 made do with one. They were at the sharp end of pent-roof combustion chamber development, but the 750 used hemispherical heads. They pioneered four valves per cylinder, but the 750 had just two. To an engineer, there was really nothing remarkable about the CB750 – except that it was a four, and it was in the shops.

No, what you got was a neat and surprisingly compact transverse four, with eight valves, one chain-driven overhead camshaft and – unlike most of its descendants – dry sump lubrication. Bore and stroke were slightly undersquare at 61 x 63mm. Primary drive was by duplex chain, and a five speed gearbox fed a peak of 67bhp to the rear wheel. It had four 28mm Keihin carbs and – above all – four brilliant chrome exhaust pipes. 'Look at me', it screamed at the world.

25 years ago, the turbine-like acceleration was a sensation. It's smooth and tractable, happy to pull away at just 1000rpm, and whirr seamless up to 9000. The effect is utterly civilised and totally anodyne, and it set the bench mark for at least two decades.

Like all performance machines, exaggerated claims were made for the Honda's performance. 115mph was the true potential. A good Norton twin was its equal, and a decent Triumph or BSA triple its better – especially when the bends arrived. What the Honda had was gentility in abundance; scarcely a single rough edge had made it into production.

With minimal vibration, no oil leaks, reliability and super-light throttle and clutch actions, the Honda mollycoddled anyone fortunate enough to step on board. On the other hand, the hydraulic disc front brake – the first on a production

motorcycle – requires considerable pressure to underwhelming effect.

The handling is mixed. Early examples, in particular, topple into corners at town speeds – in contrast to the sublime neutrality of the best of British. Otherwise, it offers impeccable walking-pace balance, and effortless 40 to 80mph cruising. Press it some more, however, and it weaves and wobbles like no British bike with sporting pretensions.

None of the CB750's handling deficiencies are primarily due to a lack of frame stiffness, although if the chassis could boast half as many tubes as the exhaust, it might handle better. The problem is distinctly limp damping mated to stiffish springing and skinny forks. The truth was that in Honda's principal market – the USA – pedigree handling was not a selling point. So why waste money designing it in?

But this is carping. The CB750 was as much a corporate vehicle as a production motorcycle; living, revving, weaving proof that a cammy four need cost little more than the price of a traditional twin (£680

Curiously understated '750' didn't say the half of it. But four pipes and silencers did the Honda's talking with chrome-plated eloquence.

in 1970). It was awesome, even to look at. Strewth, we'd never seen four silencers on *anything* before.

The other revolution was in the detailing – or sanitising – that practically everyone has since taken on board. Parts fit, precisely. Fastidious little cable guides abound, and the instruments are elegant in their one-piece neatness.

And, boy, did it sell! In the decade it was in production, from the K0 of 1969 to the last four-piper, the K7 of 1977/78, almost one million CB750s were made. *Motorcycle Sport* summed it all up at the time: 'In years to come, when historians look back on . . . motorcycling in the '70s, one of the turning points will be seen as the day when Honda made one of the most sophisticated, supposedly complicated and certainly potent motorcycles available to the public at a price it could afford.' They were right. This was, after all, the first superbike.

SPECIFICATION: HONDA CB750

ENGINE	4-cylinder 736cc SOHC
HORSEPOWER	67bhp @ 8000rpm
TRANSMISSION	5-speed
FRAME	tubular steel twin cradle
BRAKES	single disc/drum
TOP SPEED	115mph

Blue bike is the original 750-4 K0 of 1969. Golden K2 model of 1974 was re-styled but went and handled substantially the same. Almost one million were produced.

In 1968 there wasn't a word to describe it, so they invented one: 'Superbike'. Motorcycling has never been the same.

Rickman Interceptor

·····················

It began, to cut a long story short, as one of those accidents of history. 'When Royal Enfield went out of business in 1969 and left 200-odd Series II Constellation engines stranded at the docks en route to Indian in the States, someone had a brain-wave', recalls a former Rickman employee. The brain-wave was to become the Interceptor, an amalgam of Rickman's acknowledged chassis know-how and Enfield's biggest twin.

On the face of it, it's a winning combination. Visually, certainly, it's a stunner – a screaming eyeful of nickel, chrome and orange, subtle as a Hawaiian sunset and twice as blinding.

Colour aside, this was precisely the philosophy behind the Rickman brothers' – Derek and Don's – approach. The 'sixties, to quote another employee, was a time when there were 'plenty of good engines and good frames about, but it wasn't often that you got the two together'. The Rickman answer was the Metisse chassis – the name is French for mongrel bitch – to fit a variety of mainly racing engines.

To meet the Rickman maxim of 'extreme rigidity with minimum weight', the frame features a bronze-welded double cradle of 1¼ in 16-gauge Reynolds 531 steel. Eccentric chain adjusters preclude Rickman's other pet hate – inaccurate wheel alignment. The execution, as always, is superb. Even more compelling, the finished machine tips the scales at just 353lb, an astonishing 95lb less than a standard Constellation.

The first of 'around 205' Interceptors left the Rickman factory in 1970. All wore glass fibre tanks and dual seats, Borrani rims, and motocross-derived

For an accidental marriage, Rickman's Interceptor worked well. The Metisse chassis was later to prove itself capable of handling even CB750 and Z1 horsepower.

'It's a stunner – a screaming eyeful of nickel, chrome and orange, subtle as a Hawaiian sunset and twice as blinding.'

Apart from their exquisite nickel-plated frames, Rickman also developed disc brakes and their own large-diameter telescopic forks. The machine would originally have been a more muted mustard colour.

Rickman forks of a diameter – 1⅝ in (41mm) – sturdier by far than the standards of the time. Braking is taken care of by a single AP Racing caliper up front, and a rear disc of Rickman design – both ahead of their time. Indeed, the high specification of the Interceptor's standard equipment had stirred a contemporary French magazine to call it 'the Rolls-Royce of motorcycles'.

Its engine, despite Enfield's demise, was quite new. The 736cc high-cam Constellation engine had been substantially revised to become the Series II model in 1969, with twin 30mm Amal Concentric carburettors, 8.5:1 compression and higher-lift cams. The dry-sump lubrication of the Series I was superseded by wet-sump oiling, with a much-enhanced flow-rate. In typical Enfield fashion, the powerplant sat 'semi-unit' with its gearbox, the two bolting rigidly together across flat mating faces, and keeping in touch via duplex chain to a wet multiplate clutch.

Power was variously quoted as 52 or 56bhp at 6750rpm, good for a top speed of around 115mph. Best of all, the long-stroke engine is hugely tractable, with ready power from below 2000rpm. It makes even a Triumph twin feel peaky, as well as vibrating a good deal less.

The ride is light, low and agile, yet stable, precise and predictable – a rare enough combination of virtues for machines of any vintage. On the other hand, the Metisse chassis isn't altogether happy about being plucked from the race-track and plunged into duty as a sit-up-and-beg roadster. There's next-to-no steering lock, the handlebars are uncomfortably wide and the girth across the footrests simply doesn't mesh with the narrowness of the tank. For all its high-class constituent parts, the Interceptor feels slightly makeshift.

What it really begs is rear-sets and clip-ons. As a café racer, it could be peerless. As a gentleman's carriage, it affects too many compromises. Yet the build quality and redoubtable chassis of the Metisse shine through, and perhaps as small an outfit as Rickman can be forgiven for the compromises they had to make. In the overall scheme of things, outfits such as Rickman meant little, but in showing that even big bikes could handle, they paved the way for the rest.

SPECIFICATION: RICKMAN INTERCEPTOR	
ENGINE	736cc OHV parallel twin
HORSEPOWER	56bhp @ 6750rpm
TRANSMISSION	4-speed
FRAME	Metisse twin cradle
BRAKES	disc/disc
TOP SPEED	115mph

Yamaha XS-1

·························

'It's a big softie which, despite the brash claims made for it, makes little attempt to out-perform the Bonneville.'

'It's as near as you'll get to a Triumph without pushing it home every night', said the owner of this particular XS-1. Heresy? Maybe, but no more blasphemous than Yamaha's creation of the XS range of 650cc twins in the first place. Four-stroke fours and two-stroke triples were one thing, but in 1970 a machine such as this was a frontal assault on 33 years of Britishness in engine design. Vertical twins were ours, as English as eel pie, waxed cotton jackets and – yes – the Triumph Bonneville.

Indeed, the engine is what Triumph themselves might have designed if they'd had any money in 1969. Inevitably, it is in-unit, wet sump and the crankcases split horizontally. A single overhead camshaft, with the ignition points at its right end, is chain-driven from the centre of the crankshaft. Breathing was in the hands of two 38mm 'constant velocity' carbs, one of CV's earliest appearances on a production motorcycle.

Yamaha, of course, were pretty new to four-strokes at the time. The result is a sprinkling of components which look less like four-stroke parts than big RD250 bits, like the roller-bearing crank, with distinctly two-stroke-ish con-rods, running on roller big-ends. The earliest XS-1s even had needle-roller small ends.

Yamaha claimed 53bhp and 110-plus mph from the XS-1 (115mph for the later XS-2). True top speed in neutral conditions was about 105mph. Revealingly, the Bonneville, with supposedly two horsepower less, was capable of maybe 5mph *more*.

Surprisingly, considering it first appeared at the same time as Honda's CB750, the XS series did not adopt electric start until the XS-2 of 1972, which has completely reworked crankcases to accommodate the starter motor under the sump.

On the road, the engine is a delight: flexible, responsive and, thanks to rubber mounting, fairly smooth. It's a big softie which, despite the brash claims made for it, makes little attempt to out-perform the Bonneville.

Anyone expecting the best of British handling and steering, however, was in for a big disappointment. The frame, and particularly the swing-arm, probably aren't the stiffest in the world. The skinny 34mm forks and twin rear shock absorbers are patently underdamped. So, above 80mph the steering becomes vague. Throw in a few bends, bumps and cambers, and it's positively random even at speeds well below that figure. And ground clearance is poor. On the other hand it's small, not too heavy (439lb), and is manageable enough to be chucked around despite its deficiencies.

The 'Hamamatsu Bonneville' became the most successful of Japanese attempts to re-create the British vertical twin. It was ultimately bound by the same limitations inherent in the layout which confronted Triumph and BSA.

In 1970 the substantially identical similar XS-1B appeared. The first major revision was the XS-2, with a twin-piston single front disc and electric start (operated from a two-stage decompressor/starter lever on the right hand handlebar).

In 1975 the XS-650 arrived in Britain. European versions wore twin front discs, whilst the rest of the world made do with one. Frame and suspension modifications (under the guidance of British racer, Percy Tait) much improved the handling, at the expense of considerable weight. Other variants followed, until the final version was produced in 1982.

Although outwardly unremarkable compared with the likes of Honda's 750-four, the XS-1's strength was undoubtedly its engine. The 650 twin earned a reputation for rugged reliability which even big-bore sidecar motocross use couldn't dent. Neither the engine nor chassis were as sports-oriented as the best British vertical twins, nor did they possess the same pedigree. But, for all that, the XS-1 worked well in a lazy sort of way, managing to combine some of the better aspects of Japanese design with patently un-Japanese lashings of character. Heresy, perhaps – but nice.

SPECIFICATION: YAMAHA XS-1	
ENGINE	654cc air-cooled OHC parallel twin
HORSEPOWER	53 bhp @ 7000rpm
TRANSMISSION	5-speed
FRAME	Tubular twin cradle
BRAKES	drum/drum
TOP SPEED	105mph

The scene — Shaftsbury's 'Hovis Hill' — is as British as the Bonneville. The XS-1 was a comparable piece of impertinence and probably the least 'super' of the Japanese Superbikes — its frame and cycle parts were inferior to the Triumph's, whilst its engine offered only slightly more.

Laverda 750 SFC

his, more than any machine of its time, was a racer built for the street. Laverda's SFC was a raw, uncompromising beast of a machine, which even by the time it went on sale had an enviable reputation.

The Laverda factory raced only rarely. Yet in 1968 an early version of what was to become the SFC won the *Giro d'Italia* long-distance race. Three years later, an even bigger and more comprehensive triumph came Laverda's way: at the 1971 Barcelona 24-hour race, SFCs placed first, third and fourth. Not a bad weekend's work for a company which began by making tractors.

The 750 from which the SF and later the SFC was developed certainly didn't go like a tractor, but its engine was built like one. The crankshaft ran in no less than five main bearings; drive to the single overhead camshaft was by a double-row chain; and the 13-plate clutch, very heavy in operation, had its own outrigger bearing. The gearbox was similarly robust.

Although the basic configuration was much like many British parallel twins, the Laverda was thoroughly modern. As well as being overhead cam, its wet-sump crankcases split horizontally. There was electric start (a kick-start wasn't even fitted), and it didn't leak oil. And the engine's close-pitched finning, not unlike Honda's CB72, was strikingly modern. Mindful of the dodgy reputation of Italian electrical equipment, Laverda also sourced much of their components in Germany and even, later, Japan. The 36mm carburettors, though, were Spanish Amals, whilst the Italian CEV switchgear is pretty horrible.

The engine hangs from a backbone comprising four huge rails, two of which dip down to the swing-arm pivot, whilst the other two support the seat assembly and rear suspension. The engine bolts rigidly to the frame by its cam box and crankcase rear, further strengthening the design. The same overkill extends to the swing-arm which, rare for the period, is cross-braced.

Topping this off was a bright orange half-fairing and race-style 'bum-stop' seat, the latter with room for a racing number. Despite the massive engine, the silver-painted spine frame gave an impression of lightness which wasn't entirely illusory. The SFC weighed-in at 420lb, 60lb less than the SF.

SPECIFICATION: LAVERDA 750 SFC

ENGINE	744cc SOHC parallel twin
HORSEPOWER	70bhp @ 7500rpm
TRANSMISSION	5-speed
FRAME	tubular spine type
BRAKES	double drum/drum (later double disc/disc)
TOP SPEED	130mph

Although a later 500cc twin would bear the name of Barcelona's Montjuich circuit, the SFC's pedigree derived from the gruelling Spanish 24-hour race.

Early SFCs wore 230mm Laverda twin leading shoe brakes (double-sided at the front), later graduating to triple 280mm Brembo discs. Suspension, with 38mm forks from 1974, is by Ceriani. Later versions also had lighter bodywork and a magnesium rear hub, whilst their engines benefited from higher compression ratios, lighter crankshafts and a hotter 6C cam.

Although they had else little in common, the SFC was to the 'seventies what the Velocette Thruxton had been to the previous decade. Yet in contrast to the highly-strung single, the intervening years allowed the Italian machine to be both raucous and civilized (if only slightly). The SFC certainly thrives on revs – real power begins at around 6000rpm – but it is genuinely flexible and happy to dawdle at much lower speeds. Relatively smooth for a parallel twin, it is also very, very fast.

The chassis is rather less accommodating. The suspension might be fine on a smooth, purpose-built race track, but on a bumpy road any SFC is a spine-jarring experience. Clip-ons and rear-sets demand a racing crouch which soon becomes uncomfortable.

But so what? This is manifestly not a tourer. It steers accurately (and much lighter than Ducati's 750SS), handles well (far better than any contemporary Japanese superbike), and has more ground clearance than any road tyre of its vintage could exploit. It sounded like a million dollars, and looked like ten million. It wasn't for the faint-hearted, but it was special.

Just how special can easily be quantified. Of 19,000 750 Laverdas built between 1971 and 1976, only 549 were SFCs. Lucky owners.

Uncomfortable race-style riding position made hard riding almost second nature.

'It sounded like a million dollars, and looked like ten million.'

Red 1972 SFC wears large Grimeca drum brakes and Amal carbs. By 1975 (orange machine) triple Brembo discs and Dell'Orto carbs were standard.

Kawasaki 750H2

....

*I*n *Bike* magazine of November 1984, Mark Williams wrote of the H2 Kawasaki that 'here is a machine so utterly and completely dedicated to completing the distance from A to B in the fastest possible time . . . such acceleration will satisfy even the most mind-wrenched adrenalin addict'.

It was true. Here was the first mass-produced motorcycle aimed squarely at the world's nutters. These things were *ferocious*; 748cc of pure exhilaration. They'd never made two-strokes that big before. In an age still reeling from the potency of the latest quarter-litre strokers, one three times the size, in much the same state of tune, was simply – although the word wasn't so fashionable at the time – awesome.

Originally introduced as the 74bhp 750 H2 Mach IV in 1972, the H2A was, believe it or not, a refinement. The Mach IV was smoky, thirsty, peaky, wheelie-prone and evil-handling. The H2, with three horsepower less, more fork trail and a longer wheelbase, was all of the above but merely handled badly. Despite sharing the same basic engine layout, it was everything Suzuki's portly and staid GT750 was not.

Mechanically, the H2 was deceptively simple; three 250cc singles strung across the frame. Three slide-type carburettors fed in copious quantities of petrol, whilst three exhausts (one on the left, two on the right) dispensed with the proceeds and made a modest effort to quieten the ensuing racket. Almost as radical was the styling, mean and lean, with a low tank and kicked-up 'duck tail' seat, belying the machine's 450lb weight.

Everything about the machine was uncompromising. Power came in hard at 4500rpm, giving a demented surge all the way to 7000, when power trailed off abruptly. Vibration was severe at high revs. The seat was comfortable, but the high-bars and upright riding position were not. In this

For all the menace beneath, the H2 was a handsome piece of kit. Admiring it from a distance was safer than climbing aboard.

respect appalling fuel consumption, as low as 22mpg, was a blessing; stopping to fill up was a relief.

All large Japanese bikes of the period had engines which far outstripped their chassis. In the H2's case, the shortfall was extreme. The skinny frame and swing-arm flexed appallingly under load. Even the brakes could be felt bending the forks under hard braking. Kawasaki progressively extended the wheelbase between each of the three models, but never got the H2 to handle.

It was another age, another world. Kawasaki's brochure for the Mach IV heralded the triple as having 'only one purpose in life; to give you the most exciting and exhilarating performance . . .

demands the razor-sharp reactions of an experienced rider . . . a machine you must take seriously.' Try getting away with such a sales pitch these days.

By the time of the H2B of 1974, the world was no place for gas-guzzlers such as these. In three short years, the big-bore two-stroke delinquent had risen, frightened an unsuspecting world half to death, and died. We shall never see quite the like of it again.

SPECIFICATION: KAWASAKI 750H2	
ENGINE	748cc air-cooled transverse two-stroke triple
HORSEPOWER	74/71bhp @ 6800rpm.
TRANSMISSION	5-speed
FRAME	Tubular twin cradle
BRAKES	disc/drum
TOP SPEED	120mph

74bhp, a wild powerband and a chassis which would have been hard-pressed on a moped . . . only a brave man would try to use all the H2's performance. In the 'seventies, there were plenty of takers.

'The world was no place for gas-guzzlers such as these.'

The big Kawasaki triple's uncompromising nature would quite possibly be outlawed today — reason enough, perhaps, for preserving one of the most awesome chapters in motorcycling history.

Münch Mammoth

....

Take one NSU car engine, add two wheels and stir the imagination . . .

Long before Spielberg made his film, the cast list for *Jurassic Park* had already begun. The Münch Mammut (Mammoth) was quite simply the most monstrous motorcycle of the post-war years.

This Leviathan was the creation of a German, Friedl Münch, dubbed 'the Sorcerer of Ossenheim'. In the early '60s, Münch had a dream of building the most fantastic motorcycle in the world. No proprietory motorcycle engine was suitable, so Münch turned to the car world. He selected the air-cooled 1000cc unit which normally powered the NSU Prinz, enjoying considerable rally success at the time. Later versions employed a tuned 1177cc derivative of the same powerplant, and there was even a brief diversion with a three cylinder two-stroke engine.

Although an all-alloy engine, the NSU was both big and heavy. Münch's original choice of frame, a Norton Featherbed, proved too small, so he constructed a larger, beefier copy.

By then the real work had only just started. Münch made a primary drive and four-speed gearbox, both in purpose-built casings. The NSU's standard wet-sump lubrication was retained.

No ordinary cycle parts could cope with the Münch's sheer weight, so new ones had to be created. To forks of his own design Münch laced a massive 250mm twin-leading-shoe front brake which, big as it was, had trouble coping with the momentum of the 550lb machine. Much of the rest of the machine was also designed from scratch.

Like many more modern monsters – Honda Gold Wings spring to mind – the Mammoth is surprisingly well balanced once on the move. The four-cylinder engine is sublimely smooth, with a huge spread of irrepressible power which makes the four-speed gearbox almost redundant. 120mph comes easily (for the bike; with no fairing to hide behind, the rider gets a fearful battering). Claims of close to 150mph have been made for the 1177cc Mammoth Sport, but it would take a brave man to prove it.

If the Mammoth roadster was absurd, the racing version was even more bizarre. As well as a short-lived competition programme with sidecar aces Helmut Fath and Horst Owesle, in 1978 Münch attempted to beat the world one-hour record, set in 1964 by Mike Hailwood on a 500 MV.

Pretty, it was not. But as an exercise in technical overkill, Friedl Münch's monstrous creation held the motorcycling world in awe.

Cornering was never the Münch's strength, although one 125 horsepower example was raced at Daytona. The tyres, inevitably, couldn't cope.

'Claims of close to 150mph have been made for the 1177cc Mammoth Sport, but it would take a brave man to prove it.'

car engine during the period. Several road-going specials appeared, most using either the NSU unit, or the one-litre Hillman Imp engine. Both were also used in racing sidecar outfits. Some years later one bold individual even created a two-wheeler powered by a 3.5 litre Rover Vee-8 housed, oddly enough, in a standard-sized Norton Featherbed frame. More recently still, the gargantuan 'Boss Hoss' special crammed a full-blown Chevrolet Vee-8 into a motorcycle frame.

In 1972 the Münch commanded a mammoth price tag of £2500, over three times the cost of Honda's CB750. (Today, you'd need to pay perhaps eight times that for a good example). Nonetheless, about 450 were made over a period of about 15 years. The small company initially enjoyed the backing of the American motorcycle publisher, Floyd Clymer, and later from Heinz Henke. In 1977 Münch left to manufacture parts for yet another monster, the 1300cc TTS/E. But his legacy continues; the Mammoth remains the most colossal production motor-cycle ever offered for sale.

The attempt took place around the banked Daytona Speedway, using a 1370cc NSU engine with four 35mm Dell'Orto carbs and an estimated 125bhp at 8600rpm. Rider Ferdinand Kaczor had no trouble hurtling this missile through the speed trap at 178mph. However, contemporary tyre technology was simply not equal to the power and weight of the machine, nicknamed the 'Daytona Bomb', which shredded its rear cover after just three laps. A further attempt was thwarted when an American court awarded the machine to one of Münch's American backers in lieu of outstanding debts.

Nor was Münch's the only motorcycle to use a

SPECIFICATION: MÜNCH MAMMOTH	
ENGINE	air-cooled 1177cc OHC transverse four
HORSEPOWER	90bhp @ 6000rpm
TRANSMISSION	4-speed
FRAME	tubular twin cradle
BRAKES	drum/drum
TOP SPEED	125mph-plus

Kawasaki Z1

In 1972, a *grand prix* MV 500 produced around 80bhp. Then came Z1, and almost anybody could ride one on the street.

'Shutting the throttle mid-corner produced a series of violent weaves.'

Before 1972, when Kawasaki's legendary Z1 was launched, you had to be a works MV Grand Prix racer to know what 80-plus horsepower felt like on two wheels. Then Kawasaki launched the Z1, and almost anyone with £1284 to spare could share an experience only the likes of Agostini had known before.

Unlike the wild two-stroke triples which had preceded it, there was nothing particularly novel about the Z1. It wasn't the first 'modern' four (Honda's CB750 beat it to that), nor was it the first to put double overhead cams into mass production (Honda again, with the CB450). No, what the big Kawasaki did was give you more of everything, in one awesome package.

At its heart was a transverse four-cylinder engine of 903cc, fed by four 28mm Mikuni carburettors, blowing in turn into the swoopiest four-pipe exhaust system ever to pass through a chrome plater's tanks. A huge clutch housing spoke implicitly of the prodigious torque this animal could unleash.

Typical of the time, the cycle parts were less impressive. Attempting to keep the Z1 on the straight and narrow was a simple mild steel twin cradle frame which was essentially a bad copy of the Norton Featherbed of 20 years earlier. Nor was the suspension any more robust; skinny 36mm telescopic forks up front, and twin shock absorbers of doubtful damping capacity at the rear. It wasn't to be until Suzuki's GS750 of 1978 that the Japanese began to pay real heed to handling.

In the meantime the Z1 was fast – a genuine 134mph – and flawed. Ridden gently, the bike is fairly stable, with a slight tendency to understeer. Dial-in all that power, however, and Dr. Jekyll reveals Mr Hyde. You are no longer completely in control. Shutting the throttle mid-corner produced a series of violent weaves as the slack in the chassis unwound. It took a very committed rider to get the best out of the Kawasaki.

But the first impression is one of smallness for, US-style handlebars excepted, this is a low and compact device. Hit the starter, and the exhaust baffles chatter encouragingly over the breathy roar of the airbox. When the baffles quieten down, you know she's warm.

Apart from the noise and the firmness of the controls – far stiffer than the CB750, for example – there isn't as much as you'd expect to distinguish the Z1 from, say, a modern 750 Zephyr. That's how revolutionary it felt 23 years ago. Stiffest of all is the front brake, which needs a hell of a squeeze to haul down the Z1 from speed.

Tests of the time marvelled at the Z1's 'immensely strong bottom-end power', the engine's sheer durability and its reluctance to leak any oil. Above all they marvelled at top speeds well over

SPECIFICATION: KAWASAKI Z1	
ENGINE	4-cylinder 903cc DOHC
HORSEPOWER	82bhp @ 8500rpm
TRANSMISSION	5-speed
FRAME	tubular steel twin cradle
BRAKES	single disc/drum
TOP SPEED	134mph

130mph, with giddy revs and blistering acceleration, albeit only on roads with soft hedges. Even in 1995, when 82bhp is commonplace, the Z1 feels strong, eager – civilised, but with a satisfyingly raw edge that no modern retro could tolerate.

The 'true' Z1 was produced only for 1973. Rumour has it that this is the quickest example, and although its cams and exhaust are slightly noisier, this is more myth than substance. The Z1 was followed in successive years by the Z1A, Z1B and finally the much-revised Z900, before giving way to the Z1000 in 1977. In the process the machine earned a reputation for bullet-proof dependability. The fact was that the powerplant was over-engineered, for the top-end of even a 1986 GPz1100R will drop straight on to a set of Z1 crankcases. This legend was built to live on.

Over 20 years on, the Z1 remains one of the most striking superbikes to come from Japan. In contrast, all modern-day 'retros' are bland — especially when you wind open the throttle

Although Honda's CB750-4 comfortably beat it into the showrooms, Kawasaki's brutal musclebike is the one everyone remembers. Originally designed as a 750, it was punched out to 903 unforgettable cee-cee when the Honda was unveiled

Ducati 750SS

....

Not quite the real thing, but wickedly handsome and affordable: the 750 Sport.

The one that started it all: Paul Smart's Imola-winning factory 750SS. Any true 'Ducatisti', would rob banks to own it.

*W*hatever heroics Carl Fogarty, Doug Polen and the rest have achieved in recent years on their blood-red Italian twins, this is the one the connoisseurs remember. For an entire generation of bikers, this single machine launched a life-long love affair with Ducati.

Like most affairs of the heart, these ones rarely ran smooth. Twenty years ago Ducati's were cantankerous beasts with laughable electrics, fragile engines, flakey chrome and dodgy paint. 'Character', they certainly had. They also had soul.

The original soul child is Paul Smart's 750SS racer. In 1972, with no track record to speak of, this machine took on the best in the world and thrashed it hollow. The deed was done at the Imola 200-miler, just down the road from the Ducati factory in Bologna, in front of the wildly partisan *tifosi*. It was an unlikely dream come true.

In the early '70s, Ducati were known as manufacturers of lightweight racing machines – technically intriguing but well to the rear of the large-capacity horsepower race then blooming.

Then, in 1970, the Bolognese factory announced an official return to racing, with a desmodromic 500cc Vee-twin. Alongside the Colin Seeley-framed 500, Ducati developed a 750cc Vee-twin, first seen as a road-going prototype in 1970. A year later, at the Silverstone F750 round, Mike Hailwood practiced on a racing derivative of this. The bike was not competitive, and Hailwood elected instead to race a TZ350 Yamaha.

After a comprehensive winter redesign, Ducati set their sights on the 1972 Imola 200 miler, then being built up as 'Europe's Daytona'. Success would promote their new range of 750cc road bikes, but the race would be tough. No less than nine official or semi-official works teams would take part, including the brutal Kawasaki triples and Agostini on a very special 750cc MV. Briton Paul Smart, and Ducati development rider Bruno Spaggiari would pilot the machines.

Although 'very long and unwieldy', the 750 was ideally suited to Imola's fast sweeping bends. Unlike Hailwood's machine, it used standard roadster crankcases, with a wet clutch and five-speed transmission. But unlike production versions, it was pared-down for lightness, with wafer-thin bodywork, and even more fragile. Power was around 85bhp at 8800rpm.

After five laps of the 200 mile race, Smart overhauled early leader Agostini, going on to hold off Spaggiari's challenge for a sensational Ducati 1-2. At a time when Japan was obsessed with horsepower above all, victory vindicated the European approach of mechanical simplicity married to pedigree handling and a slim, wind-cheating profile, always a Ducati hallmark. Yet engineer Fabio Taglioni's development programme had touched on many forms of novelty. Fuel injection was tried, but rejected. A triple camshaft version of Ducati's unique desmodromic valve system (an additional cam lobe, rather than a spring, closes the valve), succumbed to the accountant's knife.

The big Vee-twin had first appeared as a 'street' motorcycle at the Milan Show in November 1970. By the time of the Imola victory, two production versions were available, the 50bhp 750GT, and its 'café racer' variant, the bright orange 750 Sport. With 56bhp at 8200rpm, the Sport could comfortably exceed 120mph.

The 200-miler triumph, however, spawned *the* Ducati, the 'Imola Replica' 750SS. Essentially a works racer with lights, and a great many hand-finished engine parts, only 200 were built, during 1973 and '74. (The later square-case version, built for the Italian market, is a poor relation.) Of all the Ducati roadsters ever built, this is the most prized.

Yet even as the 750SS assembly line was rolling, events were consigning it to history. The 1973 Barcelona 24-hour race brought victory for yet another prototype Duke, this time an 864cc Vee-twin. The first 860 roadster was introduced at the Milan Show, going on sale in 1975 as the 860GT. Fans of booming race replicas were not disappointed, for a few months later another Ducati classic, the 900SS, was introduced. The legacy continues today with the mouth-watering 916.

Bright orange colour scheme aside, the 120mph-plus 750 Sport was almost indistinguishable from the SS. Valves were closed by springs, however, rather than Taglioni's desmodromics.

SPECIFICATION: DUCATI 750SS	
ENGINE	748cc OHC desmodromic Vee-twin
HORSEPOWER	65bhp @ 8500rpm
TRANSMISSION	5-speed
FRAME	tubular steel backbone with engine as stressed member
BRAKES	twin disc/disc
TOP SPEED	135mph

'For an entire generation of bikers, this single machine launched a life-long love affair with Ducati.'

Yamaha RD350

··························

This is less about one particular model, than an enduring dynasty of Yamaha two-stroke twins. For 25 years from the mid-sixties, such machines captivated a generation of street riders, as well as winning more *Grands Prix* than any other manufacturer (350 from 1963 to 1990).

It wasn't always like that. In 1887 the company began making reed organs (hence their logo of three crossed tuning forks, which later became an apt metaphor for two-stroke tuning). In the 1920s they branched out into aircraft components, yet it was not until 1954 that they produced their first motorcycle. The 125cc YA1 'Red Dragonfly' was a near-copy of the same German DKW design which had spawned the BSA Bantam. In 1975 the Yamaha Motor Cycle Company was founded as a separate concern from the still successful musical instruments business.

From the outset Yamaha placed great store by competition – winning the Mt. Fuji hill climb with the YA1 in 1954; a year later the new 175cc YC1

also won. Both machines were distinctly European in appearance, but in 1958 Yamaha produced their first 'real' model, the 250cc YDS1 twin.

The twin was notable for two things – it was the first in a series of increasingly potent 250s; and in 1961 it also led to Yamaha's first venture into factory-built production racers, the TD1. Slow and hopelessly unreliable as it was, Yamaha soon learned, and from this duo sprang an empire which was to rule for over 20 years. On the road, it led to the YDS7, and ultimately the RD and RD/LC ranges; whilst on the track it culminated in the liquid-cooled TZ series which dominated almost every 250 and 350cc race of the 'seventies and early 'eighties.

With such a wealth of achievement to chose from, it's difficult to pick a pre-eminent model, but the first of the 'RD' series, the RD350 of 1973 will do as well as any other. This was the period when the 350 was one of the most popular machines in the biggest market of all, the USA.

The archetypal Japanese two-stroke twin. A close relative of contemporary TD Yamaha racers, the RD evolved into the acclaimed LC series of the 'eighties.

Civilised in looks, but ferocious in performance when it came 'on the pipe', the RD set a new standard in two-stroke design.

A development of the YR5, with which it shared a frame and the bulk of running gear and engine components, the first RD produced a sizzling 39bhp at 7500rpm. Under the heading 'Yamaha's 350 has come a long way . . .', *Motor Cycle Mechanics* suggested that 'As a 350, it makes a good 500'. This was the essence of a light, nimble and fast machine which, ridden hard, could hold its own in practically any company.

Part of the secret, new in '73, was reed-valve induction, in which a one-way valve of flexible 'petals' prevents blow-back through the carburettor, allowing a higher state of tune. Reed valves perform much the same function as the disc valves in Bridgestone's 350 GTR, but for far less cost and complexity. Even today, this remains the most common form of induction control on Grands Prix racers.

Yamaha called their reed system 'Torque Induction', and they had a point. The 350 boasted increased top-end punch without sacrificing mid-range power. This was a two-stroke which could be pottered with ease, yet offered that same manic rush of power when the engine came 'on the pipe'. Light (315lb), with a nimble chassis, good handling and a superb new front disc brake, the RD was both a peerless scratcher and moderately civilised. The cost? Just £455 in 1973.

SPECIFICATION: YAMAHA RD350	
ENGINE	347cc air-cooled reed valve two-stroke twin
HORSEPOWER	39bhp @ 7500rpm
TRANSMISSION	6-speed
FRAME	tubular twin cradle
BRAKES	disc/drum
TOP SPEED	105mph

From the RDs – the 250cc version was near-identical – developed the liquid-cooled 'LC' range of 1980, and then the YPVS 'Power Valve' models in 1983. Both became the favoured tools of a generation of street racers, creating an entire motorcycling sub-culture just as vertical twins had done 25 years earlier. Amazingly, the YPVS350 is still made, as the RD350R, in Brazil. Some legends, it seems, refuse to die.

'This was the essence of a light, nimble and fast machine which, ridden hard, could hold its own in practically any company.'

'Torque Induction' may sound pretentious, but the reed valves the RD pioneered help power almost every current *grand prix* machine.

Norton Commando

·····························

'It literally tried to blow the cylinder head off the engine.'

Ingenious Isolastic engine mounting gave Bert Hopwood's original vertical twin a massive lease of new life. This was arguably the finest incarnation of the traditional British twin.

The Commando, in 750 and later 850cc form, was the final development of the archetypal British vertical twin. Essentially, it was yet another update of Bert Hopwood's 1948 design, in an attempt to rescue the famous Norton name from five years of financial disaster.

In 1962, partly due to the failure of the 250cc Jubilee and 350cc Navigator twins, Norton had subsided into partnership with the giant AMC group. Four years later, even worse was to follow, when AMC itself collapsed. The official receiver sold off part of the company to the Manganese Bronze Holdings group, and a new company, Norton Villiers, rose from the ashes.

Norton's new base was Andover in Hampshire, where in early 1967 a replacement for the 650 and 750cc twins was designed under a team led by Dr. Stefan Bauer. The result was the Commando, which not only wore its cylinders inclined at a new, rakish angle, but – after the violent shakes of the 750 Atlas – featured a unique form of anti-vibration measure as well.

'Isolastic' was the name given to the system, in which the engine and transmission, including the swing-arm, were isolated from the rest of the machine by a sophisticated form of rubber mounting. Novel though this was, the Commando retained the clean, lean lines of its predecessors. It was light – around 400lbs. And it claimed 58bhp – fully 9bhp more than the Atlas. Less flatteringly, it retained dated non-unit construction, with the push-rod engine separate from the gearbox. Yet the British motorcycling public warmed to it, to the extent of voting it the *Motor Cycle News* 'Machine of the Year' for five consecutive years.

Norton's anti-vibration system, although

cynically dubbed 'Knickerlastic', actually worked. But the problem was that if handling was not to suffer – the rear wheel was effectively also rubber-mounted – the Isolastic bushes had to be in absolutely correct adjustment. Unfortunately this was quite a laborious operation using steel shims, and the penalty of incorrect shimming was either poor handling, the shakes, or both. Road test examples regularly had their 'Knickerlastics' shimmed solid, which helped handling at the expense of vibration. Not until 1975 did a more convenient vernier adjustment system appear, on the 850 Mk2A.

Even more troublesome was the Commando's other weakness, its crankshaft. Certain models, notably those with the highly-tuned 'Combat' engine, broke crankshafts and/or destroyed main bearings at an alarming rate. The high-compression Combat engine was also notorious for blowing head gaskets – it literally tried to blow the cylinder head off the engine. Although both problems were later solved, the Commando's reputation was tarnished.

Flawed as it was, in many ways the Commando was the best of the vertical twins, a handsome device with a strong, punchy power delivery which could humble theoretically more powerful machines. Although the 750 was a little vague at the front, the 850 was better, and handling was quite good providing the Isolastics were correctly shimmed. And a success it certainly was; 55,000 were made, 25,000 more than all Norton's previous post-war twins put together.

An 850 (actually 828cc) Commando appeared in 1973, and a more refined Mk2A 850 a year later. The last version featured a not very reliable electric start (an even less reliable version had almost reached production several years earlier), before manufacture ceased in mid-'77. Norton went on to develop and produce a range of rotary-engined models on a very small scale, limping from crisis to financial crisis in the process. Despite some heroic racing successes, it was a tragic end for one of the greatest names in motorcycling.

'Fastback' model – this one dates from 1972 – was the raciest of the Commando line.

Commando comfortably out-sold every other Norton model of the post-war years.

SPECIFICATION: NORTON COMMANDO	
ENGINE	air-cooled 745cc (828cc) OHV vertical twin
HORSEPOWER	58bhp @ 7000rpm (65bhp)
TRANSMISSION	four-speed
FRAME	tubular steel steel cradle, Isolastic engine mounts
BRAKES	drum/drum (later disc/disc)
TOP SPEED	110-120mph

Laverda 1000-3C

'It was bold,
and it was
brutal, and it
said one thing
loud and clear
– power!'

If Laverda's 750SFC was a lot of a good thing, the 1000cc triple was almost too much. This was no mere superbike; this was a *musclebike*.

First launched in 1973, the Breganze factory's first production triple took over where the twin left off. The engine was a massive affair, its exquisite Italian castings deeply finned or just as deeply polished. It was bold, and it was brutal, and it said one thing loud and clear – power!

In the early 'seventies, even the best Grand Prix 500s developed no more than the 3C's 80bhp – yet this was a road bike. The engine responsible boasted twin overhead camshafts, three 32mm Dell'Orto 'pumper' carburettors (an extra squirt of petrol was fired into the cylinder when the twist-grip was cracked open), and the usual Laverda engineering overkill. Everything in Breganze, it seemed, was built big.

Typically, the engine had a deep, finned wet sump in crankcases which split horizontally. Less commonly, unlike the 120 degree crank layout of BSA/Triumph triples, the Laverda's two outer pistons rose together, with the middle one 180 degrees adrift. This gave the 1000 a characteristic off-beat exhaust note, as well as being credited with its thunderous response to the throttle from low rpm. Some years later Laverda adopted a 120 degree layout in pursuit of smoothness, but lost much of the engine's animal character.

Big, bold and brutal, the Breganze-built triple combined Z1-type power with much better handling.

As well as being vividly quick – geared for 138mph at 7500rpm in top gear – the 3C offered prodigious power right through the rev range. It seemed to matter little which of the five gears you happened to be in; twist the throttle, and she'd respond. Inevitably there was a price for such exhilaration. Enthusiastic riding could see fuel consumption plummet into the mid-thirties. Hard use was similarly punishing to tyres and chains; the big triple was never a cheap machine to run.

This ruggedness was echoed by everything else about the 1000. It's a big machine, weighing over 530lb ready to roll (473lb, dry). At 31½ inches, the seat was particularly tall for its day. The controls, especially the clutch, are heavy, although a plus point was adjustable handlebars and footrests, which still haven't become the norm.

Although the big Laverda never handled as well as Italian sports contemporaries from Ducati and Guzzi, it was pretty good. At low speeds, the steering is distinctly odd, a feature accentuated by the standard fitment of a steering damper. The handling, not surprisingly, is heavy, although the 3C steers accurately and can chop line mid-corner. It is scarcely nimble, but a wheelbase of 58½ inches wasn't excessive. One of the penalties imposed by the wider engine was in ground clearance; the alternator cover could be made to ground on the right.

Early examples of the triple – 3CE in Britain – came with wire wheels and drum brakes similar to the 750SFC's. 1975 versions adopted twin front

Brembo discs, whilst the later 3CL sported cast wheels and disc brakes all round. Even with a fuelled-up weight of over 530lbs, disc-braked versions were sensational in their stopping power. Brembo simply had no equal at the time.

Our time frame doesn't quite permit us the ultimate triple, the 1000 'Jota' developed by British Laverda importer Roger Slater. The original Jota, sold from 1976, featured higher compression pistons, wild camshafts, bigger carbs (without air cleaners) and a tuned exhaust system. This added 10bhp to the 3C's 80bhp, and created a 140mph legend – the Fastest Production Roadster in the world. It was the ultimate man's machine; a superbike that needed Supermen to tame it.

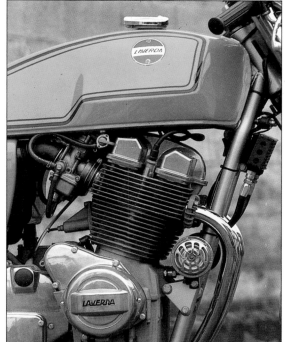

Tuned 'Jota' version of the 3C was originally developed by the British Laverda importers and rapidly became a world-wide legend.

SPECIFICATION: LAVERDA 1000-3C	
ENGINE	Air-cooled 981cc DOHC transverse triple
HORSEPOWER	80bhp @ 7250rpm
TRANSMISSION	5-speed
FRAME	tubular twin cradle
BRAKES	double disc/drum
TOP SPEED	132mph

The original muscle machine, Jotas were raced with as many as *three* steering dampers.

BMW R90S

Where the rest chased cams and cylinders, BMW's 'seventies Superbike stuck to its roots to produce arguably the best sports tourer of its time. 100mph cruising, with luggage, was effortless for rider and machine.

The R90S first launched by BMW in the South of France in 1973 was arguably the first true superbike in a range of horizontally opposed shaft-drive twins dating back precisely 50 years. In fact, in their haughty and independent way, it wasn't until the 'seventies that the German factory seemed remotely concerned with what the rest of the motorcycle world might be doing. Yet when they did pay heed, the result was a memorable motorcycle.

The R90S was a stablemate of the 6 Series BMWs first sold in 1974, which were themselves a five-speed up-date of the 5-Series twins of 1969. The range comprised the 600cc R60/6, 750cc R75/6 and 900cc R90/6.

The mid-seventies, of course, was the time when the superbike race was gathering unprecedented momentum. In designing the 90S, Bee-eM deliberately set out to enter the fray. But inevitably their contestant would do things the Bavarian way. The engine was basically the same push-rod 898cc unit fitted to the R90/6. Bigger 39mm Dell'Orto carburettors and high compression pistons pushed power up to 67bhp.

By the time it appeared, the R90S was a non-starter – numerically, at least. Compared to the contemporary Kawasaki Z1, it had 15 less horsepower and a top speed perhaps 10mph slower. It had a 'mere' two cylinders, yet cost a great deal more. But, typically BMW, it had an extra something. It placed function higher than fashion, and so somehow amounted to more than the sum of its parts: the holistic motorcycle.

Perhaps the most crucial of these, a real novelty in 1973, was a handlebar-mounted 'bikini' fairing. It wasn't big, it probably wasn't particularly aerodynamic, but it did permit you to hold a high speed for far longer than on any Japanese four.

The seat, too, was comfortable – not very sexy, but welcomed by any rider with a long journey ahead of him. The suspension was more compliant than any other road machine of the time, and the ergonomics as a whole were unequalled. Add a fuel capacity well in excess of five gallons, a smooth engine (if not as smooth as smaller BMW twins), and a flexibility far greater than the Z1's, and the result was the mile-eater *par excellence*. The R90S was the Pullman carriage of 'seventies superbikes, a by-word for effortless long-distance capability.

The 90S also handled far better than large Japanese bikes of the period. With soft, long-travel suspension, it wasn't quite so taut as the best sports machines from Guzzi or Ducati. But it made the most of its relatively low overall weight (around 430lb) and the low centre of gravity inherent in the flat twin design. In the 'seventies you could have suppleness or you could have handling, but you

Although one of the most capable long-haul machines ever built, the R90S also tolerated scratching better than many subsequent BMWs. Its relatively light weight and a punchy, flexible engine came into their own on back roads.

couldn't have both – but the big Beemer came pretty close. And, thanks to twin Brembo front discs, it delivered class-leading stopping power.

Then there was the special factor that went some way to justifying a price tag of almost £2000, half as much again as the Z1. The finish, in classy silver/black or silver/orange 'smoke', was superb. Build quality was similarly in the Rolls Royce league. Yet the machine, with its wonderfully accessible engine layout, was simplicity itself to work on. And, most of all, it contributed to BMW's peerless reputation for mechanical reliability.

Of course the other defining quality of this 'ultimate' flat twin is that no-one else produced anything quite like it. BMWs are simply unique, which itself is reason enough to aspire to owning one. Ironically, during the 'eighties even BMW

themselves attempted to drop the range until thwarted by a world-wide clamour of indignation. They're still there, in original and four-valve form. For flat twins are as Bavarian as beer festivals and *lederhosen* – except that all 90S models were actually built at Spandau, Berlin. But this was still, for many, Bavaria's best-ever twin.

SPECIFICATION: BMW R90S	
ENGINE	Air-cooled OHV 898cc flat twin
HORSEPOWER	67bhp @ 7000rpm
TRANSMISSION	5-speed
FRAME	Tubular steel twin cradle
BRAKES	Double disc/drum
TOP SPEED	125mph

'BMWs are simply unique, which itself is reason enough to aspire to owning one.'

Moto Guzzi 750S

'Like all Guzzi vees, it had that special Mandello brand of remorseless, easy power.'

Prior to the 'sixties, Moto Guzzi were best known for two wildly different engine configurations. Ever since the first Guzzi & Parodi machine of 1920, they had promoted a succession of elegant single-cylinder designs with the cylinder horizontal-mounted. At the opposite extreme, their 500cc Vee-eight of 1956 was possibly the most complex and exciting Grand Prix racer ever produced. Along the way there were other layouts – parallel twins, triples, supercharged racing fours, fore-and-aft wide-angle Vee-twins – but the horizontal single and the V8 were quintessentially Guzzi.

But not any more. Mandello del Lario is now home to the most enduring range of Italian Vee-twins in motorcycling.

It is part of motorcycling mythology that the Vee-twin engine which has powered big Guzzis for almost 30 years began life as the powerplant for a bizarre military three-wheeler. Although only produced for four years from 1960, the 753cc six-speed '3x3' used tracked rear wheels and could almost literally climb the proverbial gable-end.

When three-wheeler production ceased, Guzzi sought another use for all that torque. The results were to become as sexy as the 3x3 had been grotesque.

In 1964, work began on the first two-wheeled prototype, under Guzzi's brilliant chief engineer, Ing. Guilio Carcano, the man responsible for *that* V8. A year later a prototype was hailed as the star of the Milan Show. The machine, now dubbed the V7, reached the shops in 1967.

To this one engine can be traced almost the whole of Guzzi's subsequent history for, more than any surviving manufacturer except Harley-Davidson, they have clung to their principles. In its original 703cc form, the twin produced some 40bhp at a leisurely 5800rpm. The engine, using many car-

SPECIFICATION: MOTO GUZZI 750S	
ENGINE	OHV 748cc V-twin
HORSEPOWER	53bhp @ 6300rpm
TRANSMISSION	5-speed, shaft
FRAME	Twin cradle, demountable lower rails
BRAKES	Twin discs/disc in Guzzi linked system
TOP SPEED	123mph

No motorcycle cobbled together in this way should be remotely this handsome — unless, perhaps, it was built in Italy. Tonti's 750S design stands out for looking good and going at least as well.

type engineering practices, was simple, remarkably solid and easy to work on. But the whole, although eye-catching with its metallic red tank with chrome knee recesses, was somewhat agricultural and heavy in appearance.

In 1967 Carcano retired. Lino Tonti, a veteran of Aermacchi, Bianchi and Gilera, took his place, and set about refining the V7. The first results were the V7 Special and Ambassador of 1969, both now with 757cc, bigger valves and 45bhp. Tonti was also later responsible for taking the engine up to 844cc for the GT850 and California of 1972.

Tonti's real breakthrough, however, came with the V7 Sport. His background was in lighter, leaner machines than the early Guzzi vees, and he set about remodelling the V7 in similar mould. By transferring the generator from the top to the front of the engine, he produced a machine which was both lower and sleeker than before, yet with more ground clearance. At the same time he added a fifth gear and reduced the capacity slightly to 748cc to permit the machine's use in increasingly popular 750cc racing.

The result, much refined and no less than 28kg lighter than the first V7, was the V7 Sport of 1972. A high-performance 'Le Mans' version, with half fairing and 'bum-stop' racing seat, was even more exhilarating (and brought the promise of the true Le Mans series which was to arrive in 1976). Like all Guzzi vees, it had that special Mandello brand of

By the 'seventies, handling was an Italian speciality. Firms such as Moto Guzzi showed the Japanese there was more to motorcycle design than simply putting a potent engine between two wheels.

remorseless, easy power. But now it was so much more *alive*.

Yet even here Tonti was not finished, for two years later he unleashed the 750S, now with two huge 300mm Brembo discs up front. Finished in all black with violent red, orange or green flashes across the tank and side panels, it was the most eye-catching machine of its era. In mid-'75 this became the 750 S3, with milder cam timing but the same 53bhp at 6300rpm. Now with a rear disc brake, the S3 adopted Guzzi's unique linked brake system. It was to be the last of Guzzi's sports 750s. And in more ways than one, it was the ultimate.

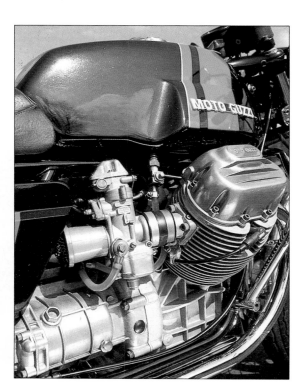

First developed for a bizarre military vehicle, much the same Guzzi powerplant survives today. But the 'seventies, when it was competitive for speed, was its hey-day.

Suzuki GT750

. . . .

'At 90mph-plus, even the mildest motorway curve is likely to invoke a weave.'

Rod Morgan's GT750B, was the last of the breed when first registered back in '78. The B's most obvious distinguishing feature is the lack of stays on the chrome front mudguard.

In the days before anyone had even dreamt of emissions regulations, Suzuki's GT750, nicknamed variously the 'water kettle' and 'water buffalo', was the two-stroke answer to Honda's CB750. And to everyone's surprise it was the stroker which became a by-word for easy-going grunt, whilst the four-stroke Honda launched the tide of rev-happy multis which surrounds us still. Yet just five years earlier, Suzuki were working on a 50cc racing triple which revved to 19,000 and didn't have enough gears with 14.

For the time, the technical specification was mouth-watering; three liquid-cooled cylinders mounted transversely across the frame, mated to a five-speed in-unit gearbox by geared primary drive. The engine is piston-ported, and fed (in final versions) by three 40mm CV carburettors. With a chrome three-into-four exhaust, and very wide across the crankshaft, the engine was physically imposing. Less advanced by far, was the chassis.

Launched in 1971 as the GT750J, the Kettle enjoyed a much shorter model run than its Honda counterpart. The J was notable for its fade-prone drum front brake, lurid paintwork and four curious silencers whose black end-cones were adept at falling off, shortly followed by an ungodly racket as the baffles followed suit. The J was succeeded by the short model run of the 750K, substantially the same bike but with much-needed twin discs up front. The styling was somewhat in the manner of Wurlitzer.

1974 brought about the slightly less baroque GT750L. A year later the M appeared, with the 70bhp engine which was to last the Kettle until the end of its days. Compared to the previous 65bhp/112mph motor, the M was about eight mph faster and somewhat revvier, but still a big softy at heart. Perhaps it had become embarrassing to Suzuki to have a pussy-cat on the street, when its racing derivative (the machine crashed so spectacularly at Daytona by Barry Sheene) was such a tyre-shredding missile on the tracks.

Instead, the GT majored on effortlessness and – unprecedented for a two-stroke – longevity. This was due to a modest rev ceiling of 7000rpm, and liquid cooling, which promoted durability by minimising temperature gradients and piston clearances. And everything was built big.

In this respect the Kettle was a complete success, regularly clocking mileages previously unheard of for two-strokes. Maintenance, too, was simple, with just occasional gearbox oil-changes and ignition points to look after. Ironically it was the electrics, rather than the engine, that usually proved the weak link when Kettles did break down.

But most of all the triple was appealing – and still is – for the way it went. Not only was it better braked and far more tractable than the Honda four, and easier to get away from the lights, it was smoother, too.

The handling, though, is distinctly mixed. Ridden with prudence, it's an attractive package. Although it feels much bigger and heavier than the CB750, the difference is actually only a few pounds. At town speeds it steers more neutrally, with far less

tendency to fall into turns and crisper low-down power.

At higher speeds, things get interesting. At 90mph-plus, even the mildest motorway curve is likely to invoke a weave. Ground clearance, although better on later versions, was slight. Even 'conveniences' like a digital gear indicator and vacuum-controlled fuel tap can't conceal the fact that getting anywhere quickly is a bit of a lottery.

The GT750 enjoys a unique place as not only the first, but the last of the big two-strokes, a demise jointly ensured by rising oil prices and increasing concern over emissions. When Suzuki announced what was to be the last of the Kettles in late '76, the writing on the wall, unveiled at much the same time, was the GS750, Suzuki's first big four-stroke multi. Apart from looking about a hundredweight lighter (it wasn't; only 25lb), the GS set the standards for the next generation by doing something the GT never could – it handled.

Huge and imposing, the 'Water Kettle' was the opposite of other road-going two-strokes: flexible, relaxed and reliable. But rising fuel prices sidelined large capacity strokers almost overnight.

SPECIFICATION: SUZUKI GT750	
ENGINE	liquid-cooled 3-cylinder 738cc 2-stroke
HORSEPOWER	70bhp @ 6500rpm
TRANSMISSION	5-speed
FRAME	tubular steel twin cradle
BRAKES	twin disc/drum
TOP SPEED	120mph

Kawasaki KR750 Racer

·····················

*I*f the 'sixties was the decade of the screaming tiddlers, the 'seventies was the Animal Decade, the years of Formula 750, of brutal horse-power, skinny tyres and flexi-frames. From 1972 to 1978, Kawasaki's roadster-based triples, along with the even grosser Suzuki GT750s, were the quintessential racing superbikes. The example pictured, Mick Grant's 1976 KR750, was the ultimate development of the breed.

Surprisingly, Grant enjoyed riding his KR. 'At the time', he recalls, 'the press dubbed it an animal, but it was very rideable and extremely competitive, if not initially very reliable. The Suzuki's were definitely more of a handful, Yamaha's TZ750 was a jelly by comparison, and both were much heavier than the Kawasaki.' This particular machine, the only one ever made with magnesium crankcases, is the lightest KR ever built.

Grant's first outing on a KR was Daytona in 1975, when 'disastrous' gearbox problems prevented the machine ever completing more than five laps at a time. The KR's biggest handicap, however, was its over-stressed crankshaft. On early models, the fancy aircraft-type fuel quickfiller was of limited use, since the crankshaft lasted little longer than a tank of petrol. A crank life of 90 miles was a particular problem in the F750 world championship series, since most races were over 100 miles. Later examples, with improved crank design and peak revs reduced from 10,000 to 9500rpm, proved more robust.

Whatever its shortcomings, the KR had made immense strides since the introduction of its predecessor, the H2R, in 1972. The H2R was a heavily-tuned version of the 750cc H2 roadster (see page 70), retaining both the road bike's air-cooling and, more crucially, its blood-curdling handling.

Paul Smart, who rode in the Kawasaki America squad alongside Yvonne du Hamel and Art Bauman, remembers the H2R as 'absolutely atrocious . . . awful handling, totally unreliable'. Although it is Barry Sheene who will always be remembered for being spat down the road when his rear tyre cried enough, most riders had a similar experience. Despite this, and a process of 'constant de-tuning', Smart topped the US road race standings in 1972. Yet the HR2 was only really

tamed after Smart later had Colin Seeley build a frame for it, when it handled 'superbly'. Effective as it was, this 'defection' earned Smart no friends at Kawasaki.

In 'standard' tune, the KR's peak power was claimed as 120-plus bhp, with pulling power 'like a tractor'. A second-stage tune, involving different pipes, a 2mm shorter piston skirt and higher compression, gave perhaps 130bhp and was the practical limit of the KR's potential. Only once, at the ultra-fast Mettet circuit in Belgium, was Stage 3 attempted. Four mm off the piston skirt, lots of special porting and an even more radical exhaust produced an engine 'like a switch – either on or off. Completely unridable'.

Yet even in standard trim the KR750 was amazingly rapid. In 1975 Grant added no less than 7mph to the lap record for Ireland's NW200 circuit. At Macau in 1976, Grant lapped everyone except the runner-up. In winning the 1978 Isle of Man TT

'It was very rideable and extremely competitive, if not initially very reliable.'

on this very bike, he was speed-trapped at over 190mph. The figure has been questioned, even by Grant himself, yet KRs regularly clocked 180mph at Daytona, without the downhill advantage of the TT speed trap. Only in the last few years have *Grand Prix* 500s come to exceed those figures.

Despite this the big Kawasaki never quite achieved its potential. It's fragility prevented it ever mounting a convincing assault on the F750 title, although riders like Hansford, du Hamel, Ditchburn and Grant enjoyed the occasional success. When Yamaha put their full might behind their factory OW31, the KR's days were numbered.

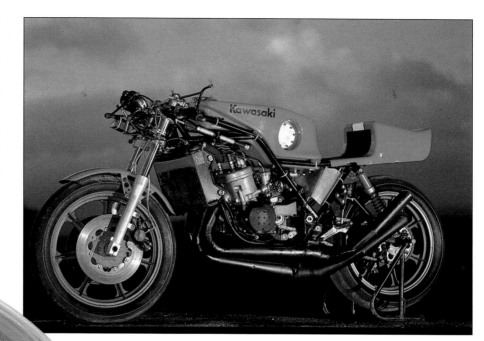

SPECIFICATION: KAWASAKI KR750 RACER	
ENGINE	liquid-cooled 748cc two-stroke triple
HORSEPOWER	120bhp-plus @ 9500rpm
TRANSMISSION	5-speed
FRAME	tubular steel twin loop
BRAKES	double disc/disc
TOP SPEED	180mph-plus

Green only in colour, the 190mph Kawasaki triple (above) could shred tyres and lap records with equal vigour — just so long as the crankshaft held together.

Picture shows the final version of the green meanie, Mick Grant's magnesium crankcased KR750 of 1976. By then it had come a long way from the original modified H2 roadster.

MV Agusta 750S America

....

*I*f any manufacturer of two-wheelers emulates the uniquely Italian flair of Ferrari cars, MV, surely, is the one. When Gilera pulled out of *grand prix* racing at the end of 1957, MV went on to claim manufacturers' titles at *every class* for the next three years. Even more astonishing, MV captured the 500cc crown every year from 1958 to 1974, through riders John Surtees, Gary Hocking, Mike Hailwood, Giacomo Agostini and Phil Read. The latter, with Read fighting off the growing (and now utterly dominant) two-stroke menace, must rank as one of the most dramatic and heroic 500cc series since the world championship began in 1949.

MV was founded as an aircraft manufacturer in 1923, and four years later was inherited by Count Domenico Agusta. After World War II, he

Wickedly handsome, the vibrant red MV had the sort of glamour that even Kawasaki's much faster Z1 could not match. Almost every part of the dauntingly expensive Italian four was hand-crafted.

established the Meccanica Verghera Agusta motorcycle factory at Gallarate, near Milan. The first MV racer, a 125cc two-stroke, was built in 1948 and won the national championship. But Count Agusta had his mind on higher prizes, recruiting Gilera's Pietro Remor to design a squad of MV four-strokes. Cecil Sandford gave the Count his first GP success in winning the 1952 125cc title, a class Carlo Ubbiali was to dominate for MV in the late 'fifties. In total MV claimed 16 500cc titles, nine at 350cc, five 250cc and seven 125cc.

The 750S America is not a race bike – not quite. But as a roadster it shares with Ducati's 750SS the mantle of the first 'race replica' superbikes; raw, uncompromising, exotic and expensive, street legal (but only just). Yet MV's first four-cylinder

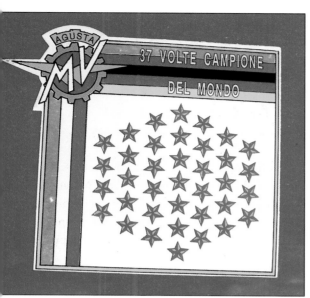

37 VOLTE CAMPIONE DEL MONDO

750S graphics (far left) trumpet MV's domination of the 500cc *grand prix* scene from 1958 to '74. But despite its racing pedigree, the shaft-drive roadster was heavy and didn't handle particularly well (left).

roadster, produced in 1967, could not have been more different. Of 600cc, it was a tourer – slow and, most unforgivable of all, ugly.

When the 750S arrived in 1971, it did much to restore MV's reputation. Good looking and fast, it was followed by the America in 1975. This, aimed at the US market, was styled to emulate the 500 on which Read had won MV's 37th (and, it turned out, last) world title the previous year. Red and silver paintwork gave the machine the look of the 'Gallarate fire engines', especially with the optional race-style full fairing.

The heart of this sensuous device, inevitably, was its 790cc four-cylinder engine – practically a scaled-up replica of the factory racers. With gear-driven double overhead camshafts, four Dell'Orto carbs (gulping unfiltered air) and four raucous straight-through megaphone exhausts, this was arguably the most exotic production motorcycle produced until Honda's NR750 came along 17 years later.

Exotic, yes, but imperfect. Despite high-quality suspension from Ceriani, the America was a disappointing handler, particularly at high speed. The fault seemed to lie with a frame design employing just a single backbone tube, and with the curious choice of shaft final drive. With a dry weight of well over 500lbs, it was also disappointingly heavy.

That engine, though, was memorable. Somewhat truculent at low speed, it found its soul through revs, emitting a piercing and unforgettable howl as the needle hurtled around the tachometer dial. Although true rear wheel horsepower was

somewhat less than the 75bhp MV claimed, it was substantially more than any other contemporary '750', rushing the red and silver MV up to 130mph and beyond. The America's successor, the 837cc, 85bhp Monza, was even more exhilarating.

The price, of course, was considerable. Even in their heyday MV roadsters were a very rare sight. Sales never met MV's expectations, and this intricate and hand-crafted machine was fearfully expensive to produce. By 1979, the company had ceased manufacturing motorcycles to concentrate on helicopter production.

'The 750S America is not a race bike – not quite.'

SPECIFICATION: MV AGUSTA 750S AMERICA	
ENGINE	air-cooled 790cc DOHC transverse four
HORSEPOWER	75bhp @ 8500rpm
TRANSMISSION	5-speed
FRAME	duplex steel cradle
BRAKES	double disc/drum
TOP SPEED	133mph

Benelli 750 SEI

....

*B*ack in 1975, you'd go a long way to see one of these. Benelli's magnificent 750's place in superbike lore is assured: the first production motorcycle to boast six cylinders.

Although the transverse six is perhaps their best-remembered creation, the business founded by the Benelli brothers in 1911 had a long and illustrious racing history. A Benelli 250 won the last pre-war Lightweight TT, whilst another repeated the success in 1950. In the same year, Dario Ambrosini brought Benelli their first world title.

Then, in 1962, Benelli produced an astonishing 250cc four, which later grew into a 350 and then a 500. Thus equipped, the little Italian factory took on the mighty Hondas and MVs. Success didn't come until Honda pulled out of Grands Prix, allowing Kel Carruthers to take the quarter-litre title in 1969, but the battle was heroically fought.

Above all, it showed that Benelli undoubtedly knew how to make multis.

The 750 *Sei*, and its stablemates, the 350cc and 500cc fours, grew out of the extravagant ambition of Alessandro do Tomaso. Do Tomaso was an entrepreneur who attempted to rationalise and modernise mass production of motorcycles in his native Italy. He also owned Moto Guzzi.

Dubbed the 'Six pipe dream' in a test of the time, the most strident result of these aspirations was the 750-6. Suddenly all those 'too complicated' Japanese multis looked restrained. Finished in bright red, seemingly as wide as a bus but with acres more chrome, the *Sei* was a sensational eyeful.

Like other multis before it, the six wasn't actually that complex – it merely duplicated a lot of its bits. A single overhead camshaft topped off a 12-valve cylinder head fed by three Dell'Orto carbs.

As an exercise in corporate *machismo* – it was Latin, after all – the *Sei* was a magnificent success. The reality, however, was flawed.

These were quite small at 24mm (compared to four 28mm carbs on Honda's 750).

The wet sump crankcases split horizontally, revealing a crankshaft with no less than thirteen plain bearings. The single overhead camshaft is chain-driven. Primary drive is by a further chain from the centre of the crankshaft, an otherwise sound piece of engineering which unfortunately puts the five-speed gearbox in a very asymmetric position. As was to become widespread practice on later fours, the alternator was mounted above the gearbox to keep engine width to a minimum.

This was all very impressive, apart from two things: if, say, Honda had built the six, the detailing and finish would almost certainly have been better and it wouldn't have wept oil, as the Benelli sometimes did. And, most tellingly of all, the Benelli wasn't actually that quick. Road tests gave top speeds as high as 118mph, but 114mph was nearer the norm.

Visually impressive as it was, basically this wasn't a very powerful engine. Most engines develop less power than their manufacturers claim, but in the six's case the shortfall was considerable. Benelli claimed 71bhp, but the truth was nearer 60. Part of the problem, it seemed, was very high pumping losses, which also contributed to oil consumption as low as 300 miles per pint. At 37mpg, it was also greedy for petrol.

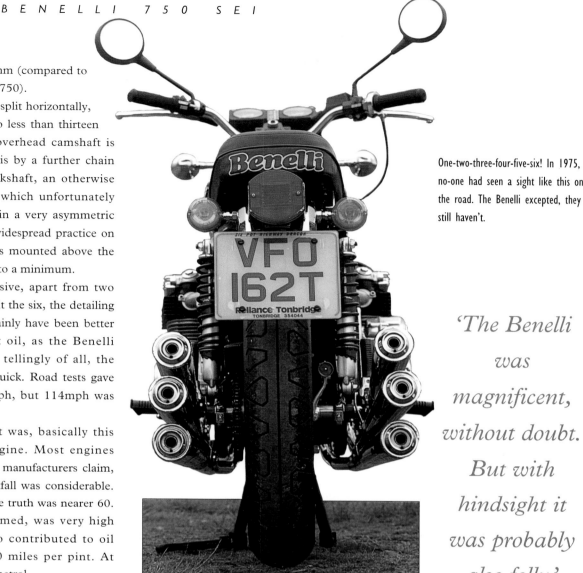

One-two-three-four-five-six! In 1975, no-one had seen a sight like this on the road. The Benelli excepted, they still haven't.

'The Benelli was magnificent, without doubt. But with hindsight it was probably also folly.'

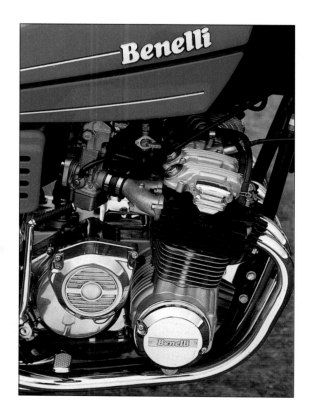

What the *Sei* did deliver was unprecedented smoothness from a revvy engine which needed all of its five gears. Although wide and heavy at 485lb, it handled and steered fairly well, and stopped superbly with its twin Brembo discs. But, smoothness aside, all of this was offered in equal or greater measure by machines costing substantially less.

Kawasaki's Z1, for instance, cost some 30 per cent less than the *Sei*, despite 20mph more top speed and over 1½ seconds advantage over the standing quarter mile. Even Honda's CB750, at little more than half the price, was faster. The Benelli was magnificent, without doubt. But with hindsight it was probably also folly.

As tiny in side-view as it is gross from the front, the six's performance was hampered by huge frictional and pumping losses and barn-door aerodynamics. (Left) Peak power was around 60bhp and performance disappointing.

SPECIFICATION: BENELLI 750 SEI	
ENGINE	air-cooled 748cc SOHC transverse six
HORSEPOWER	71bhp @ 8500rpm
TRANSMISSION	5-speed
FRAME	tubular twin cradle
BRAKES	Double disc/drum
TOP SPEED	114mph

Index

....